Author's Purpose

Cause and Effect

Classify and Categorize

Compare and Contrast

Details and Facts

Draw Conclusions

Graphic Sources

Main Idea and Details

Sequence

Steps in a Process

Literary Elements

PICTURE IT!

A Comprehension Handbook

Author's Purpose

Authors write to inform or entertain

To Inform

To Entertain

Cause and Effect

Why did it happen?

Cause

What happened?

Effect

Classify and Categorize

Which toys belong together?

Spaceships

Action figures

Compare and Contrast

How are
we alike?

How are
we different?

Details and Facts

Draw Conclusions

Use what you already know to help you understand what is happening.

Graphic Sources

Time Line

How I Get Ready for School

6:30   7:00   7:30   8:00   8:30   9:00

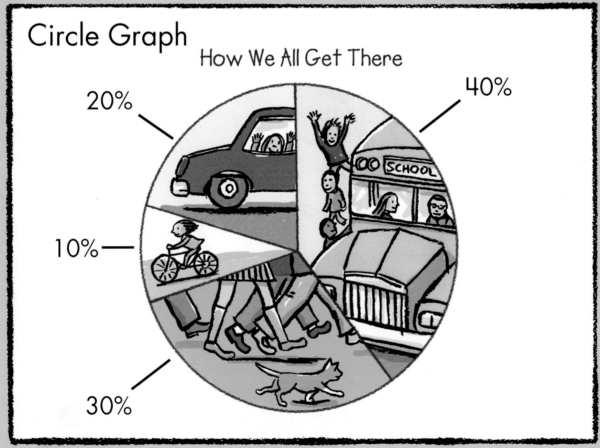

Circle Graph

How We All Get There

20%

40%

10%

30%

Main Idea and Details

Main Idea

What is the selection all about?

Details

Sequence

What happens first, next, and last?

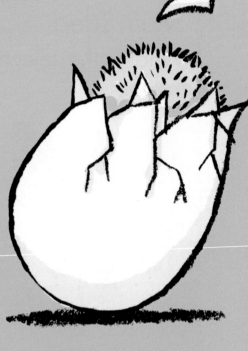

Steps in a Process

1

2

3

4

Literary Elements

Characters

Plot

Beginning

Middle

End

What happens in the beginning, middle, and end of the story?

Problem/Solution

Problem

Solution

Setting

Where and when does the story take place?

Theme

What is the big idea in the story?

Reading STREET

Program Authors

Peter Afflerbach

Camille Blachowicz

Candy Dawson Boyd

Connie Juel

Edward Kame'enui

Donald Leu

Jeanne Paratore

Sam Sebesta

Deborah Simmons

Alfred Tatum

Sharon Vaughn

Susan Watts Taffe

Karen Kring Wixson

PEARSON

Glenview, Illinois • Boston, Massachusetts • Chandler, Arizona
Shoreview, Minnesota • Upper Saddle River, New Jersey

Our Changing World

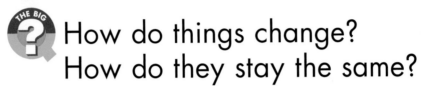

THE BIG Q How do things change?
How do they stay the same?

Responsibility

THE BIG ? What does it mean to be responsible?

Picture It! A Comprehension Handbook **PI•1– PI•13**
Words! A Vocabulary Handbook **W•1– W•15**

Traditions

 How are traditions and celebrations important to our lives?

20

Picture It! A Comprehension Handbook PI•1– PI•13
Words! A Vocabulary Handbook W•1– W•15

Contents

21

Our Changing World

THE BIG
?

How do things
change? How do
they stay the same?

UNIT 4

Our Changing World

Let's Talk About
Our Changing World

LS1.0 Students listen critically and respond appropriately to oral communication. They speak in a manner that guides the listener to understand important ideas by using proper phrasing, pitch, and modulation.

25

Build Vocabulary

Learn ◉ **Skill Prefixes** are word parts added at the beginning of words. When the prefix *un-* is added to a word, it makes the word mean "the opposite of ____." For example, *untie* means the opposite of *tie*, and *undo* means the opposite of *do*. You may be able to use the prefix *un-* to help you figure out the meaning of the word.

Practice

Read "Going West" on page 27. Try using context clues to find the meanings of the highlighted words. If you need more help, use your glossary or a dictionary. Also look for words that begin with a prefix.

Words to Know	blankets	quilt	stuffing
	wrapped	trunks	unpacked
	pretended		

On Your Own

Read "Going West" again. Write the two words from the passage that begin with *un-*. Beside each, write the base word (the word without the prefix). Now try adding the prefix *un-* to other words from the Words to Know list. Which one becomes a new word when you add *un-*? Write the word.

G3R1.7 Use a dictionary to learn the meaning and other features of unknown words.
R1.9 Know the meaning of simple prefixes and suffixes (e.g., *over-, un-, -ing, -ly*).
G1R2.4 Use context to resolve ambiguities about word and sentence meanings.

Going West

In 1844 the Wilsons headed west to Oregon. They traveled in a covered wagon pulled by two oxen. In the wagon was everything they needed for the trip. They also had everything they needed to begin their new life in Oregon.

Friends told the Wilsons to bring lots of blankets and quilts. A quilt is a cover for a bed. To make a quilt, Mrs. Wilson put cotton or wool between two pieces of cloth. Then she sewed the pieces of cloth together. This stuffing made the quilt thick and soft.

Mrs. Wilson used all of her quilts. She wrapped her dishes in some quilts. Then she packed the quilts into trunks. The trunks would not be unpacked for four months. The Wilsons used some quilts as beds. Folded quilts on the wagon seats made the hard seats softer. They hung other quilts inside the wagon to keep out the wind and the dust. Jimmy Wilson even wrapped a quilt around himself and pretended it was a cape!

 Need a Review?
See *Words!*, p. W•5 for more information about prefixes.

 Ready to Try It?
Read *The Quilt Story* on pp. 30–44.

Our Changing World

Build Comprehension

Learn ◎ **Skill Compare and Contrast**

- When you compare and contrast, you see how things are alike and different.

- Words such as *like, but,* and *both* are clues that can help you see how things are alike and different.

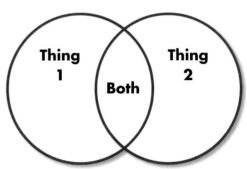

Thing 1 | Both | Thing 2

Practice Read "Celebrating Mom and Dad" on page 29. Watch for clue words that help you see how things are alike and how things are different.

On Your Own **Write to Read** Reread "Celebrating Mom and Dad" and make a diagram like the one above to show how the two celebrations are alike and different. Fill in the diagram with details. Use your diagram to write a sentence that tells how the celebrations are alike. Then write a sentence telling how they are different.

 Need a Review?
See *Picture It!* on p. PI•5 for more information about comparing and contrasting.

 Ready to Try It?
As you read *The Quilt Story* on pp. 30–44, watch for clue words that tell you things are being compared.

R3.1 Compare and contrast plots, settings, and characters presented by different authors.

Celebrating Mom and Dad

Mother's Day and Father's Day both come on Sundays. But what we do on those days is different.

For Mother's Day, Mom always gets flowers. For Father's Day, Mom makes a special breakfast with biscuits for Dad.

Mom wants us all to dress up and go out to eat on Mother's Day. But Dad always wants to stay home in old clothes and watch a game and cook outside.

We always give our parents gifts. Mom and Dad both want things that we have made. My sister and I have made pen cups, storybooks, and pictures.

I'm glad there are special days to let our parents know that we love them.

Skill Get ready to find out how Mother's Day and Father's Day are alike and different.

Skill The clue word *both* tells that the two celebrations are alike. How are they different?

The Quilt Story

by Tony Johnston

illustrated by Tomie dePaola

Genre **Realistic fiction** tells about events that could happen in real life. Read about what happens to a little girl's quilt.

How does a quilt change as time passes?

A little girl's mother
made the quilt
to keep her warm
when the snow came down,
long ago.

She stitched a quilt
by a yellow flame,
humming all the time.
She stitched a tail of
falling stars.
And she stitched the name,
Abigail.

Abigail loved the quilt.
She wrapped it round her
in the quiet dark
and watched the winter skies.
Sometimes she saw a falling star.

Sometimes Abigail
played in the woods
near her home.
She had tea.
Her dolls had tea.
And the quilt had tea
all over it.

Sometimes she pretended
the quilt was a gown.
She wore it to town
on her horse,
clop, clop, clop.
And it tore.

So her mother
stitched it up
once more.

Sometimes she played
hide-and-seek
with her sisters.
She laughed and cried,
"Don't peek!"
and hid under the quilt.
And everyone found her.

Sometimes Abigail
was sick.
She sneezed
and sneezed.
Then she slept
under the quilt.
And she felt better.

One day Abigail's family
moved away, across wide rivers
and over a rock-hard trail.

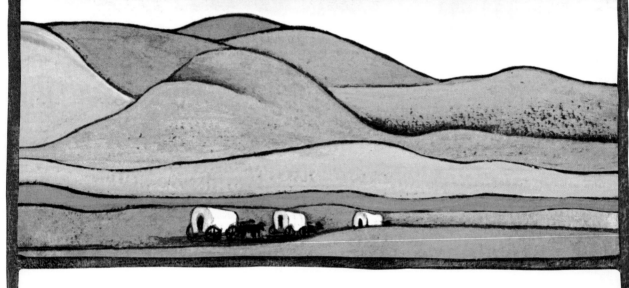

The quilt went too.
Not stuffed in trunks
with the blankets
and clothes. It kept
the little girls warm
from the wild winds.
Warm from the rain.
Warm from the
sparkling nights.

They built a new house
in the woods.
Abigail's father built it
with his hatchet,
chop, chop, chop.
He built her a new bed,
chip, chip, chip.

He made her
a new horse too.
He worked until
curly shavings
covered the floor
and everyone sneezed
and said, "Welcome
home," and was glad.
And Abigail felt sad.

New house.
New horse.
New bed.
Everything smelled of
fresh chops and chips.
Everything but the quilt.

So her mother rocked
her as mothers do.
Then tucked her in.
And Abigail felt
at home again
under the quilt.

One day when the quilt
was very old and very loved,
Abigail folded it carefully
and put it in the attic.
Everyone forgot it
was there.

A grey mouse came
and loved the quilt.
Her babies were born
on top of it.
They grew fat and grey
in the warm stuffing.
When they got hungry,
they ate a falling star.

A raccoon came and loved the quilt. She dug a hole in a corner with her black paws and hid an apple there.

A cat came
and loved the quilt.
A patchwork cat.
It rolled on the stars,
and stuffing spilled
out like snow. Then
the cat curled up in
the snow and purred.

"Kitty, Kitty,"
called a little girl.
She found her cat
and she found the
quilt, splashed with
patterns of sun.

The little girl wrapped
the quilt round her.
And she loved it too.

"Can you make it like new?" she asked her mother.

So her mother patched the holes. She pushed fresh stuffing in. She stitched long tails on the stars to swish across the quilt again.

One day the little girl's family moved away,
across miles and miles of pavement
and snaking gray highways.

They found a new house.
Freshly cleaned.
Freshly waxed.
Freshly painted. White.

They unpacked and
unpacked. All night.
And everyone sneezed
on cardboard dust
and said, "Welcome
home," and was glad.
And the little girl
felt sad.

Everything smelled of
white paint and boxes.
Everything but the
quilt. So her mother
rocked her as mothers
do. Then tucked her in.
And she felt at home
again under the quilt.

Think, Talk and Write

Talk About It What story would you tell if you were Abigail's quilt?

1. The pictures below show what happens in the beginning, middle, and the end of the story. Use them to help retell the story of Abigail's quilt. **Retell**

2. How did Abigail and the second little girl feel about the quilt? Compare and contrast their feelings. How were their feelings alike and different? **Compare and Contrast**

3. This story doesn't happen on one day. How does the author show that the story happens over a long time? **Story Structure**

Look Back and Write How does a quilt change as time passes? Use details from the selection as you write your answer.

Retell

 LS1.8 Retell stories, including characters, setting, and plot.

Author and Illustrator

Meet the Author

Tony Johnston

When Tony Johnston was young, she wanted to be a veterinarian or a "bugologist." She collected everything that flew or crawled. She even raised monarch butterflies. But when Tony grew up she became a teacher, and she sometimes wrote stories for her students. Another teacher saw her talent and encouraged her to become a writer. Ms. Johnston says, "As soon as I realized how hard (and satisfying) it was, I was hooked."

She has gone on to write more than 80 children's books. She and her family have lived in New York, Mexico, and California.

Fishing Sunday

Read two more books by Tony Johnston.

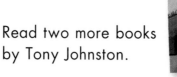

The Iguana Brothers

Meet the Illustrator

Tomie dePaola

Tomie dePaola says that his goals as a child were to write stories, draw pictures for books, and sing and tap dance on the stage. He has now done all these things.

Read two more books by Tomie dePaola.

Mr. dePaola uses his own childhood for ideas too. His Italian grandmother was the model for the grandmother in *Watch Out for the Chicken Feet in Your Soup*. He has written or illustrated over 200 books and won many awards for them. He lives in New Hampshire with his two dogs, Moffat and Markus.

Adelita: A Mexican Cinderella Story

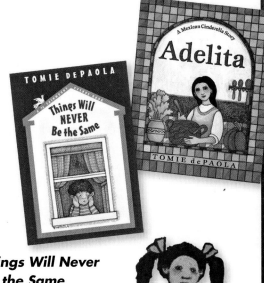

Things Will Never Be the Same

Our Changing World

Text Features help readers locate important ideas. Text features include headings, lists, charts, graphs, illustrations, and captions.

Ask and Answer Questions as you read. Begin by looking at text features. Ask yourself, "What is this selection about?" Then read to find answers.

▷ **Ready to Try It?**
Read "Making Memories: Changing with the Times." Ask questions about the text as you read. Then reread to look for answers.

Social Studies Link

Talk to your family about family history. Think about this history showing on a quilt. Then draw a picture of your quilt.

Making Memories
Changing with the Times

an interview with Mary Jane McDonald

by Myka-Lynne Sokoloff

Mary Jane McDonald tells about a special quilt she helped make. It was made for the 200th birthday of Brewster, Massachusetts.

Myka-Lynne Sokoloff: In the past, quilts were very useful. They covered beds and kept people warm. What is different about this quilt?

Mary Jane McDonald: Old quilts were made from old clothing and bits of fabric people had around their houses. The idea of buying new fabric and tearing it up seems odd to some people. It's a changing art form.

We're a long way from the kinds of quilts that were made from old dresses, old tablecloths, and old linens to use up the last bits. The pioneers used everything they possibly could. They threw very little away.

MLS: Times have changed, haven't they?

MJM: We live in a throw-away society now.

MLS: Tell me about the Brewster quilt. Who worked on that?

MJM: Anyone who lived in town could work on it.

MLS: How did you choose the pictures that would go on the quilt?

A church has been on this spot for 300 years.

MJM: We wanted to make a map of Brewster. Then we placed the map on the background. We started with the sky, then the ocean, and then sand. After that, it started to grow like weeds.

MLS: How did you choose which buildings to put on the map?

MJM: We made a list. We decided that the church was important. It started in 1700. We felt the store was important. It was a meeting place in town. We wanted to include the old and the new.

People still gather at The Brewster Store today.

Many sea captains lived in Brewster long ago. This sea captain's home is on the quilt.

MLS: You were trying to show how the town had changed?

MJM: Yes. We wanted to make it new but still show the important things from the past.

MLS: It seems like the quilt really did change over time. You really didn't have a design in mind. You didn't cut the pieces to fit a pattern. It just grew?

MJM: Yes, that's right. We decided we needed some old sea captains' houses, because this is a town of sea captains. We put in the bike path, which used to be the railroad track.

MLS: What do you hope people will learn when they look at the quilt?

MJM: Just a sense of Brewster— what it has to offer.

The quilt hangs in the town library. People may see it there 200 years from now. They will see how the town has changed.

Reading Across Texts

The quilts in *The Quilt Story* and in this interview were made for different reasons. What were the reasons?

Writing Across Texts

Make a chart that tells who made each quilt, why they made it, and who enjoyed it the most.

Writing and Conventions

Writing Realistic Fiction

Prompt In *The Quilt Story*, a quilt undergoes changes as a girl grows and changes. Think about something else a child might treasure. Now write a story about how something familiar makes things easier for a child.

Writing Trait

Good **word choice** appeals to the reader's senses.

Student Model

Brown Bear

Ty was upset. He'd had a bad day. He'd been stuck in the cold rain while waiting for the bus. At school, his favorite pencil broke.

Ty cried, "Where is Brown Bear?"

"It's right here," his mother said in a gentle voice.

"Everything will be all right now," he said.

Realistic fiction has characters and a setting.

Adjectives help us see and feel.

Writer chooses words that appeal to the senses.

W1.1 Group related ideas and maintain a consistent focus. **LC1.3** Identify and correctly use various parts of speech, including nouns and verbs, in writing and speaking. **G1W1.2** Use descriptive words when writing.

Grammar Adjectives and Our Senses

An **adjective** describes a person, place, animal, or thing. An **adjective** can tell how something looks, sounds, tastes, feels, or smells.

They moved away, across **wide** rivers.

Wide describes the way the rivers looked.

Practice Write the adjectives from the model. Write whether each adjective tells how something looks, sounds, tastes, feels, or smells.

Let's Talk About
Our Changing World

LS1.0 Students listen critically and respond appropriately to oral communication. They speak in a manner that guides the listener to understand important ideas by using proper phrasing, pitch, and modulation.

Our Changing World

Build Vocabulary

Learn   ⊙ **Skill Antonyms** are words that have opposite meanings. For example, *old* is the opposite of *new*. When you do not know the meaning of a word in your reading, try looking at the words and sentences around it. The author may have used an antonym. It can help you figure out the meaning of the unfamiliar word.

Practice   Read "Great Grapes" on page 59. Study the highlighted words. Then look for a pair of antonyms from the Words to Know list. Write them on your paper.

Words to Know	fruit	vine	soil
	root	harvest	smooth
	bumpy		

On Your Own   Read "Great Grapes" again. Find another pair of antonyms in the article. Write them on your paper. Now think of three more pairs of antonyms that you know. Add these to your list. Write a sentence using one of the antonym pairs.

R1.7 Understand and explain common antonyms and synonyms.
G1R2.4 Use context to resolve ambiguities about word and sentence meanings.

Great Grapes

Grapes are a kind of fruit. They are small and round. They grow on a vine. Grapes come in many different colors, such as green, red, white, black, and blue.

Grape farmers usually do not start with new vines. They cut and save parts of the old vines. Then they plant the parts in the soil. The vine makes a root that pushes into the soil. The farmers hang wires between poles. The vines cling to the poles and grow up and across the wires. Vines use long, thin shoots, called tendrils, to hold on as they climb. The vines do not grow grapes for several years. But once they start growing grapes, they can grow them every year for as long as 100 years!

Grape harvest happens in the summer or fall. Farmers cut the grapes from the vines. Grapes for eating are put in boxes and shipped to market. Some grapes are spread out on paper and left in the sun to dry. Soon the grapes are no longer smooth. They have become small, bumpy raisins.

 Need a Review?
See *Words!*, p. W•2 for more information about antonyms.

 Ready to Try It?
Read *Life Cycle of a Pumpkin* on pp. 62–75.

Our Changing World

Build Comprehension

Learn ⊙ **Skill Details and Facts**

- Details are small pieces of information. Details can help you picture what you are reading.

- Facts are pieces of information that can be proven.

- You can use facts and details to back up your opinions about what you read.

- As you read, try to decide which details and facts are important—which ones support a point the author is making.

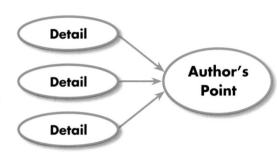

Detail → Author's Point

Detail → Author's Point

Detail → Author's Point

Practice   Read "Our Red Oak" on page 61. Watch for details that help you picture the tree the author describes.

On Your Own   **Write to Read** Reread "Our Red Oak" and make a graphic organizer like the one above. The author says this tree is the best tree in town. Write details in your organizer that support that idea. Now write about something you like best. Use details in your writing.

 Need a Review?
See *Picture It!* on p. PI•6 for more information about details and facts.

 Ready to Try It?
As you read *Life Cycle of a Pumpkin* on pp. 62–75, watch for useful details and facts.

  R2.5 Restate facts and details in the text to clarify and organize ideas.

Our Red Oak

We have a great tree in our front yard. It is a tall red oak. My dad says it is 30 feet high. Our red oak is the best climbing tree.

The branches are thick and reach toward the ground. After I climb up in the tree, I hide behind the leaves. People down on the ground cannot even see me.

I like to look at the leaves too. They are quite beautiful. Each leaf is about as long as my hand. The top part of the leaf is shiny and dark green. The bottom side of the leaf is fuzzy and brown-red in color. In the fall the leaves turn orange.

I tell friends that they can always find my house. It's the one with the best tree in town!

Skill Here the author states an opinion—the word *best* gives you a clue. The next paragraph gives facts and details to support that idea.

Skill Get ready to read some details. Can you picture how the tree looks?

Life Cycle of a Pumpkin

by Ron Fridell and
Patricia Walsh

Genre

Expository nonfiction tells facts
about a topic. Look for facts about
how a pumpkin grows.

How does a
pumpkin go
from seed
to pie?

What is a pumpkin?

A pumpkin is a fruit. It grows on
a vine like other kinds of squash. Pumpkins can be
bumpy or smooth, large or small, long or round.
They can be orange, white, yellow, or red.

Each year there is a new crop of pumpkins.
Their hard shells have deep lines that go from
top to bottom.

Seed

1 week

2 weeks

10 weeks

Pumpkins begin as seeds. The seeds are white and have an oval shape. A tiny plant is curled up inside each seed.

The seed is planted in warm, moist soil. In about ten days, a root grows down into the soil. The root takes in water and food for the plant. Tiny leaves push up into the sunlight.

11 weeks

14 weeks

16 weeks

Seedling

The first two leaves pop through the soil. These are smooth seed leaves. They use sunlight and air to make food for the new plant.

Then the true leaves appear. They are jagged and prickly. The job of the seed leaves is done. They wither and fall off.

Seed

1 week

2 weeks

10 weeks

Vine

The pumpkin plant grows more leaves. The plant grows quickly and soon becomes a vine. The vine twists and creeps along the ground.

The vine sends out thin tendrils. They grab and curl around other vines. They twist around fences. The tendrils support the vine as it grows longer and longer.

11 weeks

14 weeks

16 weeks

Flower

The pumpkin vine blooms with many yellow flowers. Some of these are female flowers. Female flowers sit on small, fuzzy, green balls.

Other flowers are male flowers. They are on long stems and have yellow powder inside the flower. The yellow powder is pollen. It takes a male and a female flower to make a pumpkin.

Seed   1 week   2 weeks   10 weeks

Pollination

It also takes bees to make pumpkins. They move the pollen from male flowers to female flowers. When a bee visits the male flowers, the pollen sticks to the bee's body and legs.

The pollen rubs off the bee as it goes in and out of the flowers. When the pollen reaches a female flower, the fuzzy green ball at the end of the flower begins to grow into a pumpkin.

11 weeks

14 weeks

16 weeks

Growing and ripening

All summer the vines, tendrils, and leaves of the plant grow and tangle together. Underneath the big leaves are little pumpkins.

The leaves are like big umbrellas. They keep the hot sun off the pumpkins. They also help to keep the soil around the pumpkins from drying out.

Seed

1 week   2 weeks

10 weeks

Problems for pumpkins

Growing pumpkins need just the right amount of water and sun. Too much rain rots the pumpkins. Too much sun withers the vines.

Cucumber beetles and squash bugs can hurt pumpkins too. Farmers spray the plant with insecticides or cover the vines with nets to protect the growing pumpkins.

11 weeks

14 weeks

16 weeks

The pumpkins grow bigger
and bigger. Inside, the pumpkins
form seeds and pulp. Outside,
the pumpkins turn from green
to orange.

Then the vines turn brown. Harvest
time has come. The farmer cuts the thick
pumpkin stem from the vine.

Seed

1 week

2 weeks

10 weeks

After the harvest

Four months ago there were only seeds. Now the farmer has harvested a wagon full of round, orange pumpkins. They will be sold at farmstands and stores.

People cook pumpkins and use the pulp to make pumpkin pie, cookies, soup, and bread. Some pumpkins are fed to farm animals.

11 weeks

14 weeks

16 weeks

Festivals

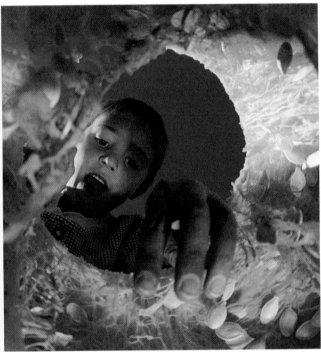

Some towns hold a pumpkin festival to celebrate the fall harvest. Sometimes there is a contest to find out who grew the biggest pumpkin.

Inside the pumpkin are many seeds. Some seeds are roasted to be eaten as a snack. Other seeds are saved to be planted in the spring. They will grow into next year's pumpkins.

Seed

1 week

2 weeks

10 weeks

Next year's crop

After the pumpkins are picked and sold, the farmer plows the field. Old vines and unpicked pumpkins get mixed with the soil. The field is ready for planting seeds again next spring.

11 weeks

14 weeks

16 weeks

Think, Talk and Write

Talk About It Discuss the instructions you would give if someone you knew wanted to grow a pumpkin plant.

1. Use the pictures below to summarize what you learned. **Summarize**

2. How are the vines and leaves important for the pumpkin to grow? **Details and Facts**

3. What questions did you ask yourself as you read about pumpkins? What did you learn? **Ask Questions**

Look Back and Write How does a pumpkin go from seed to pie? Use information from the selection to write your answer.

Summarize

R2.4 Ask clarifying questions about essential textual elements of exposition (e.g., *why, what if, how*).
R2.5 Restate facts and details in the text to clarify and organize ideas

Meet the Authors

Ron Fridell and Patricia Walsh

Ron Fridell and Patricia Walsh are married, and they are both writers. They often write their own books, but they wrote *Life Cycle of a Pumpkin* together.

Mr. Fridell and Ms. Walsh do lots of research. They use the library and the Internet, but they like to see things themselves too. When they were doing research for this book, they went to a pumpkin festival in Illinois.

Mr. Fridell and Ms. Walsh love to travel. "We travel for adventure and the excitement of seeing new places. But we also travel to do research and get ideas for our books."

Read two more books by Ron Fridell and Patricia Walsh.

Life Cycle of a Spider

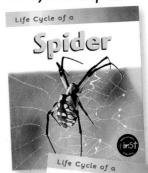

Life Cycle of a Turtle

Rhythm and Rhyme
are important parts of
some poems. To find the
rhythm, clap your hands
as you read. For rhyme,
look or listen for words
that end the same. They
are usually at the ends
of lines.

 Ready to Try It?
Read "How do seeds know
which way is up?" Look and
listen for the rhythm
and rhyme to help you
enjoy what you read.

Science Link

Try writing your own
poem about how plants
grow. Your poem might
rhyme or it might not.
If you wish, read your
poem aloud for the class.

78

How do seeds know which way is UP?

by Amy Goldman Koss

It's dark underground
Where sunlight can't go,
So how does a seed
Know which way to grow?

The root is the first
To grow from the seed—
Down into the darkness
It digs at full speed.

Gravity sensors
Within each young root
Teach it to follow
A straight downward route.

And once this young root
Has taken the lead,
A tender green shoot
Sprouts out of the seed.

The shoot only knows
That its life's pursuit
Means heading the opposite
Way of the root.

Since shoots need the sunlight
To live and to grow,
They force themselves upward
Through dark dirt below.

The roots need the water
And the shoots need the light.
Each goes its own way,
And that works out just right!

Reading Across Texts

How is the plant in this poem like the pumpkin plant you read about in *Life Cycle of a Pumpkin*?

Writing Across Texts Draw a diagram of a seed sprouting into a plant. Label your diagram.

Writing and Conventions

Writing Expository Nonfiction

Prompt *Life Cycle of a Pumpkin* tells how pumpkins grow and change. Think about something else in nature that changes. Now write an explanation of how it changes from season to season.

Adjectives describe number, size, and shape.

Writer chooses words that make the writing interesting.

Expository nonfiction gives facts and details.

Student Model

The Changing Tree

A tall oak tree grows from one round acorn. It stretches to the sky, full of leaves.

But in the fall, the leaves change. They turn many colors and fall from the tree. The big tree stands all winter without leaves.

In a few months the green leaves begin to grow back.

W1.1 Group related ideas and maintain a consistent focus. **LC1.3** Identify and correctly use various parts of speech, including nouns and verbs, in writing and speaking. **G1W1.2** Use descriptive words when writing.

Grammar Adjectives for Number, Size, and Shape

Words for number, size, and shape are **adjectives.**
The words **a** and **an** are also **adjectives.**

In **ten** days, **an oval** seed grows **a tiny** root.

Ten describes how many days. The word **an** describes
how many seeds—one. **Oval** describes the shape of
the seed. The word **a** describes how many roots—one.
Tiny describes the size of the root.

Practice Look at the model.
Write the adjectives that describe
the number, size, or shape
of something.

Let's Talk About
Our Changing World

LS1.0 Students listen critically and respond appropriately to oral communication. They speak in a manner that guides the listener to understand important ideas by using proper phrasing, pitch, and modulation.

Build Vocabulary

Learn ◎ **Skill Unfamiliar Words** are words you don't know the meanings of. What can you do when you don't know the meaning of a word in your reading? You can look at the words and sentences near the unfamiliar word. These are called context clues. Context clues can help you figure out the meaning of an unfamiliar word.

Practice Read "Working with Soil" on page 85. Try using context clues to find the meanings of the highlighted words. If you need more help, you can use a dictionary or your glossary.

Words to Know	seep particles	jagged texture	grains substances

On Your Own Read "Working with Soil" again. Did using context clues help you understand the new words? Write each highlighted word, along with the clue that helped you know its meaning. Now write some sentences of your own. Use a word from the Words to Know list in each sentence.

G1R2.4 Use context to resolve ambiguities about word meanings.
G3R1.7 Use a dictionary to learn the meaning and other features of unknown words.

Working with Soil

When I was little, I loved to make mud pies. I remember putting soil in a little red pail. Then I added water and watched it seep through the soil and make mud. I would use my thumbs to make a jagged piecrust edge to the mud pie. Sometimes I put grains of sand over the top of the pie, like sugar. When I showed my mother my mud pie, she would pretend to eat it. I would pour out the old mud until only a few particles were left in the bottom of the pail. Then I would start putting soil and water in my pail again until the texture was just right.

That was many years ago but I still make mud pies! Now it is my job to work with dirt. I help farmers by finding ways to make the soil better for growing plants. I try adding different substances to soil. Sometimes I add things, like grass or leaves. Then I see how long it takes these things to decay. Farmers depend on people like me. I find the best ways to prepare soil for planting seeds.

❚❚ Need a Review?
See Words!, p. W•7 for more information about using context clues to find the meanings of unfamiliar words.

▶ Ready to Try It?
Read *Soil* on pp. 88–105.

Build Comprehension

Learn · **Skill Graphic Sources**

- Graphic sources are ways of showing information visually, or in a way you can see.

- Some kinds of graphics are pictures, diagrams, charts, and graphs.

- Before you read, look through the story or article for graphics. Think about how the graphics might help you understand what you read.

Practice · Before you read "Good to Grow" on page 87, preview the graphic. Read the title and captions on the diagram. Look at the picture to see how the parts fit together. Then read "Good to Grow."

On Your Own · **Write to Read** Reread "Good to Grow" and look again at the soil diagram. Now write two facts you learned about soil. Share your facts with a partner.

Soil

 Need a Review?
See *Picture It!* on p. PI•8 for more information about graphic sources.

Ready to Try It?
Before you read *Soil*, look at the graphics and think about how they will help you understand what you read. Now read *Soil* on pp. 88–105.

  R2.5 Restate facts and details in the text to clarify and organize ideas.
R2.7 Interpret information from diagrams, charts, and graphs.

Good to Grow

Have you ever wondered where dirt comes from? Dirt, or soil, starts out as rock. Over many, many years, the rock breaks down into smaller pieces. These pieces become part of the soil. If you could dig until you hit bedrock, you would dig through all the layers shown in the diagram.

In places such as Central Valley, California, the bedrock layer was made long ago by a volcano. Volcanic soil contains many nutrients. Nutrients are things plants need to live and grow. In a place with volcanic soil, you will probably see many farms. In fact, Central Valley farms grow much of our country's food.

Skill This is a good place to stop reading and look at the diagram again. If you do not know what *bedrock* is, you can find out from a caption in the graphic.

Skill A diagram uses words and pictures to explain an idea. First read the title and captions. Then study the picture. What can you learn from this diagram?

Soil Profile

1 Topsoil is where plant roots are. This layer has some small sediment and a lot of organic matter, like dead leaves.

2 Subsoil has less organic matter and more sediment.

3 Bedrock is the solid rock of the Earth.

Soil

by Sally M. Walker

 **Genre**

Expository nonfiction tells facts about a topic. Look for facts about soil.

What will you learn about dirt?

What Is Soil?

Did you ever make mud pies when you were little? If you did, soil was one of the ingredients you used. You may have called it dirt instead of soil.

Soil is in lots of places. You can find soil under the grass. It surrounds tree and flower roots. It lies beneath sidewalks and streets. If you could lift your house, you would probably find soil under it too!

A scoop of soil contains many things. Soil has rocks in it. Plants and bits of leaves are in soil. Many creatures live in soil too.

Soil is a natural resource. Natural resources are materials found on Earth that help living things. They are made by nature, not people. Soil helps plants and animals grow. They cannot live without it. But where does soil come from?

How Soil Forms

Soil is made up of different kinds of materials. One of these materials is bits of rock. Rocks are broken pieces of bedrock. Bedrock is the layer of solid rock that covers the outside of Earth.

Rocks are hard. But they can be broken into tiny bits. Tiny bits are called particles. Water, ice, and wind are strong enough to break rocks.

Rocks Become Soil

Hard rocks can break into small pieces.

Ice split this huge rock in half!

As water rushes down this hill, it breaks off bits of rock.

Rushing water in rivers makes rocks roll and tumble. The rocks break into smaller pieces. Tiny particles of rock break loose.

Rainwater seeps into cracks in rocks. If it gets cold enough, the water freezes. It becomes ice. Ice takes up more space than water. So the ice pushes against the rock. It makes the cracks bigger. Pieces of rock break off.

This glacier is flowing downhill. As it moves, it carries rocks with it.

Glaciers are giant, moving slabs of ice. Glaciers are very heavy. Their weight slowly grinds big rocks into small pieces.

Wind blows sand grains against big rocks. The sand grains scrub off particles of rock.

Rocks are made of minerals. A mineral is a hard substance made in nature. Minerals are not alive, like plants or animals. The minerals in a rock become part of the soil when the rock breaks apart.

Minerals are an important part of soil. They add nutrients to soil. Nutrients are substances that help living things grow. Soil contains nutrients that plants and animals need to stay healthy.

Copper nugget

Chalcopyrite

There are many kinds of bacteria. They live nearly everywhere on Earth. This picture shows one kind of bacteria that lives in soil.

Humus is the second material that is in soil. Humus is dark brown or black. It is made of bits of dead plants and animals.

Humus is made by bacteria. Bacteria are tiny living things. They are so tiny that they can be seen only with a microscope. Microscopes are tools that make small things look big.

Bacteria eat dead plants and animals. They break the plants and animals into tiny pieces. The pieces become humus. Humus contains nutrients that had been inside the plants and animals. The nutrients can become part of the soil.

Air is the third material in soil. Soil is full of air spaces. Some air spaces are large. You can easily see them. You can see the tunnels that earthworms dig in soil. An earthworm's hole is filled with air. Soil also has tiny air spaces. The tiny spaces are between bits of minerals and humus. Most of these spaces are too small for you to see. But they are there.

Water is the fourth material found in soil. Water can move around in soil. It trickles through the soil's air spaces. The moving water picks up nutrients from the soil. The water carries the nutrients into roots of plants.

As earthworms move through the soil, they make tunnels.

Soil forms on flat land. It forms alongside rivers. It forms on forest floors and on low hills. Soil forms as humus and rock particles begin to pile up. It can take hundreds of years for 1 inch of soil to form.

Soil cannot form in some places. Soil cannot form on steep mountains. That's because soil-making materials slide down the mountain. Soil cannot form in very windy places or places where water flows quickly. In these places, soil-making materials can't pile up. They do not have enough time to become soil.

What Soil Looks Like

Soil can be made of many different kinds of minerals. Different minerals can be different colors. The minerals and humus in soil help give the soil its color. Many soils are a shade of brown. But some are yellow. Some are even bright orange red.

Soil also has different textures. Texture is how rough or smooth something is. The texture of soil depends on the size of the soil's particles.

This picture shows sandy soil (left), loam (middle), and clay soil (right).

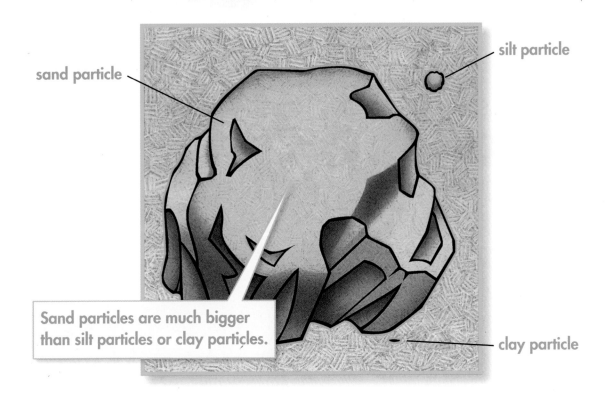

sand particle

silt particle

Sand particles are much bigger than silt particles or clay particles.

clay particle

The largest mineral particles in soil are called sand. You can see the mineral particles in sandy soil. Sand particles feel rough when you rub them between your fingers. Some sand-sized particles have sharp, jagged edges. Others are mostly round.

Another kind of particle in soil is called silt. Silt particles are much smaller than sand particles. It's hard to see silt particles. If you rub silt between your fingers, it feels smooth. Silt-sized particles are shaped like sand particles.

Clay particles are the smallest particles in soil. They are too small to see without a microscope. Clay particles are flat.

Water drains quickly through sand. That's why you won't see puddles in wet sand at the beach.

Sand particles have big air spaces between them. Water drains quickly through the spaces. So puddles rarely form in sandy soil. Silt particles have smaller spaces between them. Water takes longer to drain through small spaces. Flat clay particles get squeezed together. The spaces between clay particles are tiny. Water has a hard time trickling through tiny air spaces. Clay particles also soak up water. So it takes a long time for water to drain through soil that has a lot of clay.

Water drains slowly through clay particles. When it rains, puddles often form in the soil that has many clay particles.

Soil with equal amounts of sand, silt, and clay particles is called loam. Loam is very good for growing plants. It holds just the right amount of water for growing roots.

Soil that has mostly sand-sized particles is called sandy loam. Water drains quickly through sandy loam.

Soil with mostly clay-sized particles is called clay loam. Water drains slowly through clay loam. Rain often forms puddles in clay loam.

What kind of texture does your soil have? Rub the soil between your fingers. Does it feel rough, smooth, or in-between?

Put some soil in your palm. Add a small amount of water to your soil. Add only enough to make the soil moist. If it seems too wet, add a little more soil. Mix the soil and water together with your fingers. See if you can mold the soil into a flat circle. If you can, your soil has a lot of clay. If the circle crumbles, the soil contains more sand and silt than clay.

The next time you go outside, look at the soil around you. Notice its color. See what kinds of plants are growing in it. Feel its texture.

Watch how people take care of the soil. Try to think of ways that you can care for the soil around your house. Plants, animals, and people will always need healthy soil!

Think, Talk and Write

Talk About It Discuss the different types of dirt and soil you have seen and where you have seen them.

1. Use the pictures below to summarize what you learned. **Summarize**

2. Look at the diagram on page 101. What does the diagram compare? **Graphic Sources**

3. Make a word web. In the center of the web write *Soil.* In the outer circles of the web, write words that are related to soil. **Graphic Organizers**

TEST PRACTICE

Look Back and Write Look back through the selection. Write about why soil is important to people and animals.

Summarize

R2.5 Restate facts and details in the text to clarify and organize ideas. **R2.7** Interpret information from diagrams, charts, and graphs. **W1.1** Group related ideas and maintain a consistent focus.

Meet the Author

Sally M. Walker

Sally M. Walker has won several awards for her writing. Most of her books are nonfiction. She especially enjoys writing about science. She says, "I enjoy finding odd snippets of information that get children 'turned on' to science."

Ms. Walker lives and writes in Illinois with her husband, two children, a golden retriever, and two cats.

Read more books by Sally M. Walker.

The 18 Penny Goose

Bessie Coleman Daring to Fly

Burrowing Animals

by Penny Dowdy

Gophers and Prairie Dogs

Gophers are small, round animals. They have very small eyes and ears. Their bodies are covered with brown fur, but their tails are nearly bare. A prairie dog is a small, short-tailed animal. Like the gopher, it has small ears and eyes.

Gopher

Prairie Dog eating grass

The prairie dog has lighter brown fur than the gopher and a much shorter tail. Prairie dogs get their unusual name from the barking sound they make. Gophers and prairie dogs both eat grasses and other tender plants. They help keep the soil healthy and loose. Gophers and prairie dogs are food for animals such as hawks, owls, and foxes.

Prairie Dog

109

Gopher and prairie dog burrows are not the same. A gopher burrow can be 100 feet long or more. Gophers also build 6–12 mounds

Prairie Dog Mound

in their burrows. The mounds let them go in and out when they need to. Gopher mounds are very well hidden. Covers on the mounds keep the burrows dark and keep other animals out.

Prairie dog mounds are large and easy to see. They leave their mounds open. The holes in the mounds let them watch for animals that may be hunting them. Prairie dogs also like wind and light coming into their burrows.

Burrowing Owls

Some surprising animals live in burrows. Burrowing owls live in prairie dog or gopher burrows. But if an owl can't find a ready-made burrow, it will scratch out one of its own.

Burrowing Owl

Burrowing owls are smaller than most other owls. They may be only 10 inches tall and weigh less than half a pound. These birds have brown and black spots on their feathers and long legs.

Most owls hunt only at night. But during the day, burrowing owls hunt for insects. To make catching insects easier, the owls gather animal droppings. They put the droppings around the opening of their burrows. The droppings attract bugs. Then the owls can easily catch bugs to eat. Then at night, they hunt for small animals.

Burrowing Owls

Reading Across Texts

Soil gives lots of facts. Think about them and decide whether any would be important to a burrowing animal.

Writing Across Texts Write a paragraph as if you were a burrowing animal. Tell how soil facts are important to you.

Writing and Conventions

Writing Expository Nonfiction

Prompt *Soil* tells how different kinds of soil are formed. Think about what you learned about soil. Now write a description of the soil in your neighborhood.

Student Model

The Dirt in My Neighborhood

The dirt in my neighborhood is dry. Water sinks right in. This means there is a lot of sand in the soil. In some places the dirt is sandier than in other places. The dirt in my backyard is darker than the dirt at the park.

Expository nonfiction gives facts and details.

Writer uses different sentence lengths.

Adjectives compare types of soil.

W1.1 Group related ideas and maintain a consistent focus. **G3W2.2** Write descriptions that use concrete sensory details to present and support unified impressions of people, places, things, or experiences.

Grammar Adjectives That Compare

Add **-er** to an adjective to compare two people, places, or things. Add **-est** to an adjective to compare three or more people, places, or things.

Gravel is **bigger** than sand.

Gravel is the **biggest** sediment.

Bigger compares two things—gravel and sand.

Biggest compares many types of soil.

Practice Look at the model. Write the adjectives that compare. Then write the form of that adjective that compares three or more things.

Let's Talk About
Our Changing World

LS1.0 Students listen critically and respond appropriately to oral communication. They speak in a manner that guides the listener to understand important ideas by using proper phrasing, pitch, and modulation.

Build Vocabulary

Learn ⊙ **Skill Multiple-Meaning Words** are words that have more than one meaning. Sometimes when you read, you will see a word you know, but it doesn't seem to make sense in the sentence. Perhaps there is another meaning. For example, *store* can mean "a place where things are sold." *Store* can also mean "to put something away."

Practice Read "Moving Tips" on page 117. Think about the meaning of each highlighted word. Also look for words that can have more than one meaning. Remember to use nearby words to figure out the new meaning. If you need more help, use a dictionary.

Words to Know	trouble	block	strong
	giant	fair	tears
	chuckle		

On Your Own Read "Moving Tips." What multiple-meaning words did you find? Make a list and write the meanings beside each word. Then write your own sentence using one meaning of each word. Work with a partner to share what you learned. Ask your partner to tell which meaning of the word you used in each sentence.

G3R1.7 Use a dictionary to learn the meaning and other features of unknown words.
R1.10 Identify simple multiple-meaning words.

Moving Tips

Most people don't like to move. They don't like the work and the mess. They don't like the changes they have to make. But here are some tips that can make moving less trouble.

1. Find out about the area you are moving to. Drive around the block. Look for a grocery store, the library, and other places that are impotant to you.

2. Give your new address and telephone number to your family and friends.

3. Hire strong movers. Don't try to pack and move everything yourself.

4. Put a giant label on every box that tells in which room the box belongs. Put a label on each room too.

5. Know that some things will go wrong. Maybe it's not fair, but it's true.

6. If you feel like bursting into tears, take a break. Remember, someday you will look back and chuckle about this.

▐▐ Need a Review?
See *Words!*, p. W•10 for more information about multiple-meaning words.

▶ Ready to Try It?
Read *I Like Where I Am* on pp. 120–135.

Our Changing World

Build Comprehension

Learn ◎ **Skill** **Plot and Theme**

- Every story has a "big idea." To understand a big idea, ask yourself, "What is this story all about?"

- A plot is what happens at the beginning, middle, and end of a story.

Story Map for Plot

Beginning	→	Middle	→	End

- Characters' actions make up the plot of a story.

Practice Read "The Best Summer" on page 119. As you read, think about what the girls learn about friendship. This will help you understand the big idea of the story.

On Your Own **Write to Read** Reread "The Best Summer" and use a story map to tell the most important events in each part of the story. Now write a paragraph that tells the plot and the big idea of "The Best Summer."

 Need a Review?
See *Picture It!* on pp. PI•12–PI•13 for more information about plot and theme.

▶ **Ready to Try It?**
As you read *I Like Where I Am* on pp. 120–135, watch for important plot events and the "big idea" of the story.

   G1R3.1 Identify and describe the elements of plot, setting, and character(s) in a story, as well as the story's beginning, middle, and ending. **G3R3.4** Determine the underlying theme or author's message in fiction.

The Best Summer

Tara and Crystal were drawing chalk pictures on the front sidewalk.

"Let's draw all the fun things we will do this summer." Tara said. The girls made pictures of day camp, swimming, picnics, roller-skating, jumping rope, and watermelon.

"This will be a great summer!" Crystal said.

Skill You have read the beginning of the story. What has happened so far?

The next week, things changed. Crystal fell and broke her arm. Her arm was in a cast, and it hurt. Tara made her friend a get-well card.

"No picnics, no swimming," said Crystal. "No day camp, no roller-skating, and no jumping rope. This will be a bad summer!"

Skill Crystal feels disappointed because her plans didn't work out. Have you ever felt this way? Read on to find out what makes Crystal feel better.

Tara went to see Crystal every day. The two girls played games. They made a tent out of a blanket. They talked and laughed. The girls sat on the steps and ate watermelon. Crystal said, "You are my best friend, Tara. This is a good summer after all."

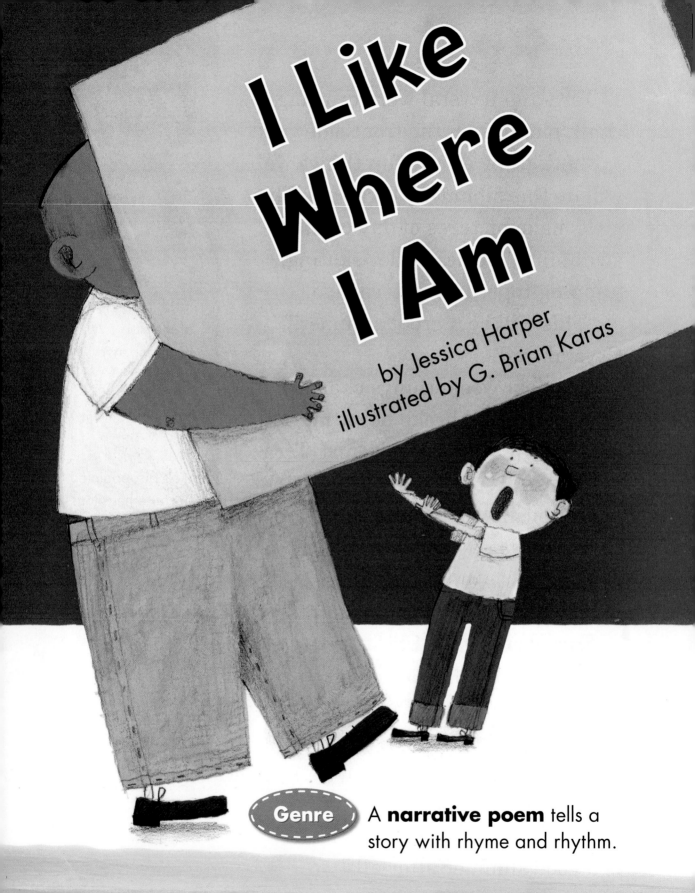

I Like Where I Am

by Jessica Harper

illustrated by G. Brian Karas

Genre A **narrative poem** tells a story with rhyme and rhythm.

What would make the boy say, "I like where I am"?

121

I've got Trouble. . . . . .
    I've got

BIG TROUBLE . . . . . .

'Cause I'm sittin' in my house
    on Willow Street
And I love this house.
    I love this street.
A prettier house
    you'll never meet
And I like where I am.
Yes, I like where I am.

That's why I've got Trouble.

'Cause I'm just kinda, you know, sittin',
Just messin' around with Mimi's kitten.
That's Mimi over there,
        in the little red chair.
She's usually got food in her hair.
She's not even two,
        so it's really not fair
That she's got a kitten
        and I don't.

And I'm six.

Well, anyway . . .
I'm sittin' with a kitten
        and a piece of string,
Just listening to my mama sing:

"La la, la la, la la!"

And I like where I am.

pots

La la, la la, la la!

125

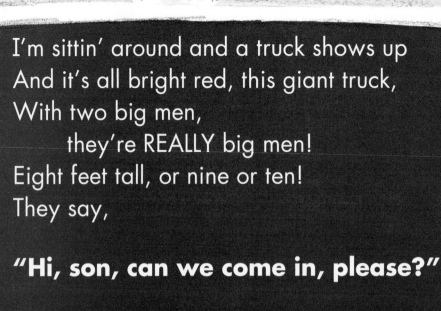

I'm sittin' around and a truck shows up
And it's all bright red, this giant truck,
With two big men,
    they're REALLY big men!
Eight feet tall, or nine or ten!
They say,

"Hi, son, can we come in, please?"

Two men, as big and strong as trees. . . .
They make me feel all wobbly-knees!
They say,
    "HI, SON!"
        and that means me,
And that means I've got Trouble. . . .

127

They say, **"Hey, son, it's moving day!"**
That's right, it's moving day.
They're gonna pick us up and take us away.
And I think (but I'm too scared to say),
Oh, why don't you just go away!
Take your truck and take your Trouble and
Move somebody else!

Move
somebody
else!

'Cause I like my room and I like my school,
And we live real close to a swimming pool,
And my best friend lives around the block.
Why move to a place called Little Rock
Anyway?

129

The two big men kinda chuckle at me,
With a **ho ho ho** and a **hee hee hee**.
My mama takes me on her knee
And sings a gentle song to me.
She rocks me back and forth.

"La la, la la, la la."

We watch the men walk back and forth
With a **ho ho ho** and a **hee hee hee**.
My tears drop down on Mama's knee.

131

They pack all our stuff in their truck—
There goes Mimi's rubber duck!
They take my bike and then my mama's.
Look! They've got my dad's pajamas!

"Everything goes!"
they say with glee,
With a **ho ho ho** and a **hee hee hee**,
And I know I've got Trouble!

'Cause I like my room and I like my school.
We live real close to a swimming pool
And my best friend lives around the block.
Why move to a place called Little Rock
Anyway?

But we did . . . . . . just like that.

And guess what?

Do you know what?

We moved to a place called Little Rock
And my new friend lives
    just up the block!
He even has a swimming pool.
My room's okay and so's my school. . . .
And I've got my own kitten!

I still think of Willow Street.
The memory is very sweet.
I'll always love where I was born . . .
But when I wake up in the morning,
I like where I am!

With a **ho ho ho** and a **hee hee hee**.
I like where I am!

Think, Talk and Write

Talk About It Has anything like this happened to you or someone you know? What would you say to someone who is moving and does not want to move?

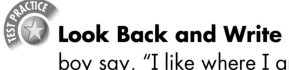

1. Use the pictures below to help you retell the poem. **Retell**

2. What happened to the boy in the poem? What do you think the theme or big idea of the poem is? **Plot and Theme**

3. How did the boy react to the news about moving away? Why do you think he reacted this way? **Draw Conclusions**

TEST PRACTICE

Look Back and Write What would make the boy say, "I like where I am"? Use facts from the poem to help you write an answer.

Retell

LS1.8 Retell stories, including characters, setting, and plot.

Meet the Author and Illustrator

Jessica Harper

Jessica Harper moved twice as a child. "When I wrote this book about moving day, I recalled how it felt as a child to have my world taken apart and put back together again." Ms. Harper enjoys writing in rhyme. She says, "It's like solving a puzzle. What's the best way to say what I have to say and make it rhyme?"

G. Brian Karas

G. Brian Karas has illustrated many children's books. In elementary school, he was known as the "class artist."

Read two other books by Jessica Harper and G. Brian Karas.

I'm Not Going to Chase the Cat Today! by Jessica Harper

Home on the Bayou: A Cowboy's Story by G. Brian Karas

E-mail These pages show what e-mail looks like on a computer screen. E-mail is short for "electronic mail." E-mail can be sent over the Internet from one computer to another.

 Ready to Try It?
As you read "A New House," use the illustrations along with the text to learn how e-mail works.

Social Studies Link

You have learned you can send messages to friends or family with e-mail. Ask your parents how they sent messages when they were young. Also talk about other ways in which their lives were different. Make a Venn diagram to compare the two time periods.

A New House

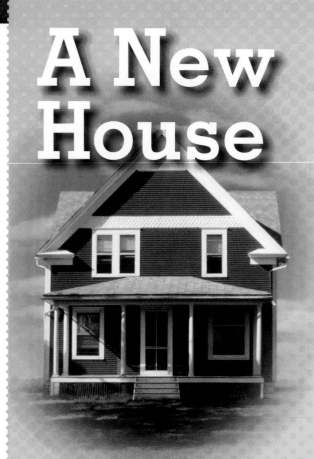

The boy in *I Like Where I Am* moved to a new home. Changes like this can be difficult but exciting.

Writing an e-mail message can help you keep in touch with family and friends far away. Here is how e-mail works.

for more practice

Get Online!
PearsonSuccessNet.com

When you turn on your computer and go into your e-mail, you can do these things.

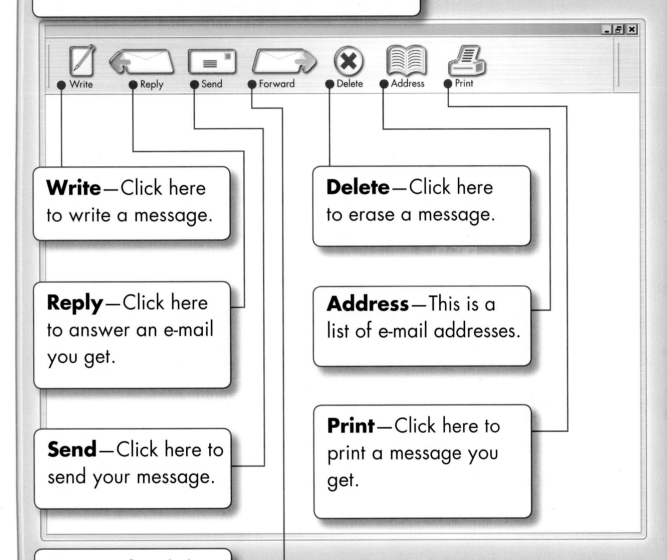

Write—Click here to write a message.

Reply—Click here to answer an e-mail you get.

Send—Click here to send your message.

Forward—Click here to send a message you get to someone else.

Delete—Click here to erase a message.

Address—This is a list of e-mail addresses.

Print—Click here to print a message you get.

139

How to Send E-mail

To write and send an e-mail, you need a person's e-mail address. E-mail addresses look like this:

(name of person)@(where message is going)

The letters on the left name the person or place you are writing to. People often use nicknames or abbreviations. The symbol @ stands for the word *at*. The letters to the right of the @ sign tell where in the world the message is going.

To write an e-mail, you click on a button that says **Write** or **Compose** or **New**. A new window will open that looks something like this:

To: You type the receiver's name here.

Subject: You type the subject of your message here. It is always best to fill this in.

Now you are ready to type your message, like the one on the next page.

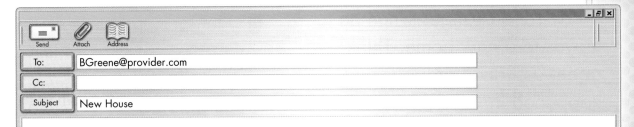

To:	BGreene@provider.com
Cc:	
Subject	New House

Hi, Beth!

What's new? If you asked me that, I'd have lots to tell you. Our new house is great. I didn't think I'd like it, but I do. I finally have my own room.

My new school is good too. I can walk and don't have to wait for a bus.

I miss you. Do you think you can come for a visit? Too bad you can't just run down the block anymore.

Your friend,

Colleen

Reading Across Texts
The boy in *I Like Where I Am* and Colleen both go through changes. Compare the changes of each.

Writing Across Texts Write an e-mail to one of them with advice about their changes.

Writing and Conventions

Writing Narrative Poem

Prompt In *I Like Where I Am,* a boy's life changes when he moves to a new home. Think about a change that has happened in your life. Now write a poem about it.

Writing Trait

Voice is the *you* in your writing.

Student Model

Wait and See

Jake came to our house today.
He can't walk or talk or play.
Why did Mama bring him here?
He is going to stay, I fear.
Maybe he'll grow up like me.
Guess I have to wait and see.

Adverbs can tell when or where.

Writer's voice is clear.

Some poems have rhyming words.

LC1.2 Recognize and use the correct word order in written sentences. **LC1.3** Identify and correctly use various parts of speech, including nouns and verbs, in writing and speaking.

Grammar Adverbs That Tell When and Where

Adverbs tell more about a verb. Some adverbs tell **when** or **where**.

Now two movers are going **upstairs**.

Now tells when. **Upstairs** tells where.

Practice Look at the poem. Write the adverbs that tell where and when.

Let's Talk About
Our Changing World

LS1.0 Students listen critically and respond appropriately to oral communication. They speak in a manner that guides the listener to understand important ideas by using proper phrasing, pitch, and modulation.

145

Build Vocabulary

Learn ◉ **Skill Multiple-Meaning Words** are words that have more than one meaning. As you read, you may see a word you know that doesn't seem to make sense. It may be a multiple-meaning word. For example, *catch* means "to grab something moving through the air," as in to *catch* a ball. *Catch* can also mean "to arrive in time for," as in to *catch* a bus. You can use the words and sentences around the confusing word to help you figure out another meaning.

Practice

Read "Amy and Jake" on page 147. Use context clues to help you learn the meanings of the highlighted words. Watch for words that have multiple meanings.

Words to Know	special picnic clung	pressing branches	fingers angry

On Your Own

Read "Amy and Jake" again. Find the word *play*. This word has many meanings, including "to take part in a game or other enjoyable activity." But this meaning does not fit the sentence. Use the words around *play* to find the right meaning for the sentence. Write the new meaning. Then write three other words you know that have multiple meanings.

G3R1.7 Use a dictionary to learn the meaning and other features of unknown words.
R1.10 Identify simple multiple-meaning words. **G1R2.4** Use context to resolve ambiguities about word and sentence meanings.

Amy and Jake

Amy and Jake are special friends. Each can do things that the other cannot. Amy can play the flute. She shows Jake how she does it—by pressing her fingers over the holes and blowing across the mouthpiece. Jake can read Braille. He shows Amy how he does it—by sliding his fingers over the raised dots.

Last summer Amy and Jake went on a picnic in the woods. Amy helped Jake climb a tree. She gave him a boost and told him where to grab the branches. As they sat in the tree together, Amy described what she saw. Jake described what he felt and heard. So it was Jake who warned Amy about the angry bees. He heard them coming long before Amy did. Amy jumped down out of the tree and helped Jake down. Jake clung to Amy's hand as the two of them ran out of the woods. They had to jump into the pond to get away from the bees. They laugh about it now, but it was not so funny at the time.

 Need a Review?
See *Words!*, p. W•10 for more information about multiple-meaning words.

 Ready to Try It?
Read *Helen Keller and the Big Storm* on pp. 150–163.

Build Comprehension

Learn ⊙ **Skill Details and Facts**

- Details are small pieces of information. Details can help you picture what you are reading.

- Facts are pieces of information that can be proven.

- You can use facts and details to back up your opinions about what you read.

- As you read, decide which details and facts are important— which ones support the author's point.

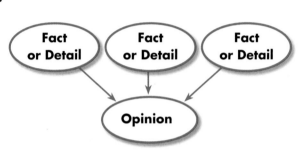

Practice Read "A Dog Named Ginger" on page 149. Think about how the author uses details and facts to support opinions.

On Your Own **Write to Read** Make a graphic organizer like the one above. Reread "A Dog Named Ginger" and fill in your organizer. Do you agree or disagree with the author's opinion that Ginger is the best dog in the world? Use facts and details as you write your answer.

⏸ **Need a Review?**
See the *Picture It!* lesson on p. PI•6 for more information about details and facts.

▷ **Ready to Try It?**
As you read *Helen Keller and the Big Storm* on pp. 150–163, watch for details and facts.

  R2.4 Ask clarifying questions about essential textual elements of exposition (eg., *why, what if, how*). R2.5 Restate facts and details in the text to clarify and organize ideas.

A Dog Named Ginger

Ginger is a very special dog. She is a guide dog. She helps people who cannot see. A mark in her ear and a tag on her collar show that she is a special working dog.

Ginger went to a training school. She learned how to walk on a lead, or stiff handle. She learned to listen. When Ginger walked with her teacher, no one could pet her, feed her, or play with her. She learned how to cross the street safely. She learned how to go around people. She learned to head through doors and up and down steps. Ginger was the best dog in her school.

Now Ginger is never afraid. She can go where her owner goes. She can ride on a bus or on a train. She can go to work and to school. She helps her owner go all around. Ginger is the best dog in the world!

Skill Ask yourself, "Why does the author think Ginger is a special dog?" When you read a fact or detail that answers your question, write it in your graphic organizer.

Skill This paragraph describes things Ginger did in her training school. Do the details help you picture what was happening?

Our Changing World

149

Helen Keller and the Big Storm

by Patricia Lakin

illustrated by Troy Howell

Genre — **Narrative nonfiction** tells the story of true events. Read about a true event from the life of Helen Keller.

What lesson does
Helen learn?

Little Helen Keller loved smelling roses and honeysuckle. They grew all around her Alabama home. But most of all, Helen loved playing pranks. When she was six, she had done her best prank yet! Mamma had walked into the kitchen pantry. Quickly, Helen felt for the key. *Click!*

Helen locked Mamma inside. Helen didn't always have the chance to take charge like that. Mamma and Papa tried hard to understand her. But many times no one knew what she wanted.

Helen could get so angry, she would kick and hit and fall into a heap. Afterward, she ran outside. She threw herself onto the cool, comforting grass. The flowers, trees, grass, warm sun, and gentle wind always made Helen feel better.

Helen was never punished for her pranks and tantrums. Mr. and Mrs. Keller thought Helen had been punished enough. Their daughter could not hear, or see, or talk. But that pantry prank forever changed Helen's life. The Kellers now knew that Helen needed more than they could give her. She needed special lessons from a special teacher.

Helen's teacher was Annie Sullivan. She came to live with the Kellers. Helen was not ready to trust this stranger. And she was not ready to give up her pranks. She locked Annie inside her room. And this time Helen hid the key! That prank made Annie see just how clever Helen was. No matter what Helen did, Annie did not give up!

Slowly, day by day, she worked with Helen. Annie taught Helen by pressing her fingers into Helen's hand. Annie's fingers spelled out the names for the things Helen loved. Grass. Flowers. Leaves. Trees. Bugs. Butterflies. Sun. Wind. Rain. In a short time, Helen loved doing her lessons more than doing her pranks.

Soon, the out-of-doors became Helen's classroom. One summer day, Helen and Annie took a long walk. On their way home, the air grew hot and sticky. Helen and Annie stopped to rest under a wild cherry tree. The tree blocked them from the burning hot sun. Its leaves fanned them with a gentle, cooling breeze.

Helen felt its strong, low branches. They were just right for climbing. Annie and Helen decided to do just that! Sitting high in the tree, they had a resting place to stay cool. It was a perfect spot for a picnic!

Annie headed for the house to make the
lunch. She made Helen promise not to move an
inch. Helen wouldn't think of moving. She loved
sitting high up in that tree! Helen breathed in the
wonderful scent of the cherry tree. She stroked its
rough bark and its smooth green leaves. She let
the cooling breeze blanket her.

But in seconds, Helen's world turned upside down. The sun disappeared. Helen's face was slapped with a cold, sharp wind.

The scent of flowers was gone. Her nose was filled with another smell. This one was not sweet. It came up from the deep, dark earth. It told Helen that a storm was near. Helen began to feel the shaking of the leaves. Twigs rained down, scratching her face, arms, and legs.

Tree limbs swayed. The wind whipped through the branches. The wind whipped around Helen. The wind tried to rip Helen right out of that tree. Helen grabbed onto the shaking branch. She clung to it with all of her might. Helen sat frozen.

She was trapped. She could not see. She could not call for help. She could not hear if help was on the way. Helen had never felt so alone or so scared. She couldn't understand how the gentle things she loved could turn against her.

Suddenly, out of the cold, whipping wind, Helen felt a hand. It was a strong, warm hand. It belonged to Annie Sullivan. Annie grabbed hold of Helen. Helen let go of the branch. She clung to Annie. She let Annie guide her down and out of that tree.

Helen learned a great deal that day. She had felt the power of Nature. It could turn from gentle to fierce in seconds. Helen also learned about the power of friendship. Annie Sullivan would always be there for Helen Keller.

Helen Keller and Annie Sullivan were friends all of their lives. Helen went on to become a talented writer who always worked to help others.

Think, Talk and Write

Talk About It On page 159, the author says, "Helen's world turned upside down." What does that mean? Explain why you think the author said that.

1. Use the pictures below to summarize what you learned. **Summarize**

2. How did Annie Sullivan help Helen Keller? **Details and Facts**

3. What questions did you ask yourself as you read? How did that help you? **Ask Questions**

Look Back and Write Look back at page 162. The author tells you what Helen learned that day. What two things did she learn? Use details from the selection to write your answer.

Summarize

R2.5 Restate facts and details in the text to clarify and organize ideas.

Meet the Author

Patricia Lakin

never saw herself as a writer. "I never thought I could write." Then Ms. Lakin took a writing class. She was told to write about things she cared about. Writing was fun for the first time.

Ms. Lakin wrote *Helen Keller and the Big Storm* because Helen had so many things to overcome. "Nature was a source of comfort for her." After being caught in the storm, Helen was shocked "to learn that nature could also be so strong and dangerous."

Read two other books by Patricia Lakin.

Dad and Me in the Morning

Snow Day!

Graphic Sources are ways of showing information visually, or in a way you can see. Expository nonfiction often uses diagrams and photos to help the reader understand the topic.

Wind

by Marion Dane Bauer

The Earth we live on is a spinning ball. When Earth spins, the air around it moves too.

▶ **Ready to Try It?**
Before you read "Wind," look at the photos and diagram. Think about what information might be given in the text. Then read "Wind."

Science Link

Use an encyclopedia or the Internet to find out more about hurricanes or tornados. Draw a diagram that shows how the storm forms. Label your diagram.

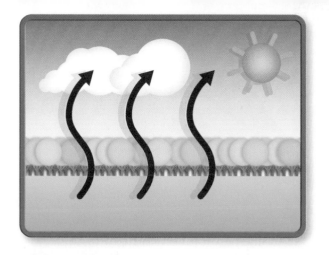

When air moves, we call it "wind." As the sun heats the air, the air grows lighter. Light air rises.

Cool air is heavy. It falls. Cool air and warm air are always trading places. We call this movement "wind."

Birds use wind to help them fly. Plants use wind to carry their seeds.

We use wind to fly kites, to sail boats, and to turn windmills.

Wind moves clouds. Wind makes waves. It even makes trees bend. When the hot air is very light and the cold air is very heavy, wind can blow up a storm!

Sometimes wind spins like a puppy chasing its tail. A small spin makes a dust devil or a water spout. A strong spin makes a tornado or a hurricane.

dust devil

view of hurricane from space

tornado

Wind can be scary. Or it can sing a gentle song. Wind is all around us, but we cannot see it. We can only see what wind does.

Reading Across Texts

In "Wind," you read: "Wind can be scary. Or it can sing a gentle song." Was that true in *Helen Keller and the Big Storm*?

Writing Across Texts

Write a short paragraph explaining your answer.

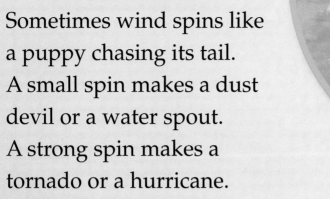

Writing and Conventions

Writing Narrative Nonfiction

Prompt In *Helen Keller and the Big Storm,* a powerful windstorm whips across the countryside. Think about a storm you have experienced or heard about. Now write a narrative about that experience.

Student Model

The Blizzard

There was a huge blizzard last Saturday. It dumped three feet of snow on our town. The snow fell slowly at first. Then it came down quickly in the afternoon. My parents unhappily shoveled the sidewalk. We all ran outside eagerly with our sleds.

Details focus on a main idea: a blizzard.

Adverbs tell how the snow fell.

Narrative nonfiction tells about a real experience.

W1.1 Group related ideas and maintain a consistent focus. **LC1.3** Identify and correctly use various parts of speech, including nouns and verbs, in writing and speaking.

Grammar Adverbs That Tell How

An **adverb** can tell more about a verb by telling **how** an action is done. **Adverbs** that tell **how** usually end in **-ly.**

> **Quickly**, Helen felt for the key.

The word **quickly** tells how Helen felt for the key.

Practice Look at the model. Write the adverbs that tell how.

Responsibility

What does it mean to be responsible?

UNIT 5

Responsibility

Let's Talk About
Responsibility

LS1.0 Students listen critically and respond appropriately to oral communication. They speak in a manner that guides the listener to understand important ideas by using proper phrasing, pitch, and modulation.

e All Writers

Bb Cc Dd
Gg Hh Ii Jj
Oo Pp Qq
Vv Ww Xx

2
70

Responsibility

Build Vocabulary

Learn ◉ **Skill Suffixes** are word parts added to the ends of words to change their meanings. You can use the meaning of a suffix to help you figure out what an unfamiliar word means. Two common suffixes are *-ly* and *-ful.*

When the suffix *-ly* is added to a word, it usually makes the word mean "in a _____ way." For example, *kindly* means "in a kind way."

When the suffix *-ful* is added to a word, it usually makes the word mean "full of _____." For instance, *hopeful* means "full of hope," and *careful* means "full of care."

Practice Read "A Trip to the Fire Station" on page 177. Think about the meaning of each highlighted word. Also watch for words that end with suffixes.

Words to Know	station	quickly	tightly
	masks	burning	building
	roar		

On Your Own Read "A Trip to the Fire Station" again. Write all the words you find that end with the suffixes *-ly* and *-ful.* Did you find five words? Use the meaning of each suffix to help you write the meanings of the words.

🐻 **R1.9** Know the meaning of simple prefixes and suffixes (e.g., *over-, un-, -ing, -ly*).

A TRIP TO
THE FIRE STATION

Carlos is a firefighter. Some children are at his fire station for a tour. He points out where the firefighters sleep and eat. Carlos slides down the fire pole. "That is how we quickly get from our beds to the trucks," he says.

"We use powerful hoses to spray water on a fire," he says. "Fire hoses can be very heavy when they are filled with water. We have to grip the hoses tightly."

"Fires give off a lot of harmful smoke," Carlos tells the children. "We must wear air tanks and masks if we go into a fire. We use masks to breathe clean air."

Carlos shows the children his thick clothes, heavy boots, and hard helmet. "These keep me safe from the things that can fall from or in a burning building."

Suddenly, the fire alarm goes off! Carlos tells the children good-bye. He puts on his gear and climbs onto the fire truck. With a loud roar, the fire truck races off.

 Need a Review?
See *Words!*, p. W•6 for more information about suffixes.

 Ready to Try It?
Read *Firefighter!* on pp. 180–193.

Responsibility

Build Comprehension

Learn   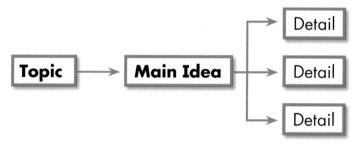 **Skill Main Idea and Details**

- Sentences that tell about the same idea are grouped together in a paragraph.
- The topic of a paragraph is a word or two that tells who or what the paragraph is about.
- It is often stated in a sentence.
- Details tell more about the main idea.

Topic → Main Idea → Detail / Detail / Detail

Practice   Read "My Uncle, the Firefighter" on page 179. Reread the third paragraph. What is the topic? To find the main idea, ask, "What is the most important idea?"

On Your Own   **Write to Read** Reread "My Uncle, the Firefighter." Then use a graphic organizer to see how the first paragraph is organized. Fill in the topic and main idea and then find three supporting details.

 Need a Review?
See *Picture It!* on p. PI•9 for more information about main idea and details.

 Ready to Try It?
As you read *Fire Fighter!* on pp. 180–193, watch for main ideas and details.

  R2.4 Ask clarifying questions about essential textual elements of exposition (e.g., *why, what if, how*). **R2.5** Restate facts and details in the text to clarify and organize ideas. **G3R2.5** Distinguish main idea and supporting details in expository text.

My Uncle, the Firefighter

My Uncle Ernie works hard as a firefighter in our town. He puts out brush fires and house fires. He helps at car wrecks. He saves people.

One morning, Uncle Ernie took me to the fire station. I saw the hose truck and the ladder truck. Uncle Ernie let me try on his heavy coat, helmet, and boots. I got to stand on the back of the fire truck! Then the firefighters had a drill. They practiced with the hoses.

Later, a firefighter named Jack told me a story. "Your uncle is very brave," Jack said. "He went into a burning house to get people out. When he saw their dog inside, he went back in to rescue it." I was very proud of Uncle Ernie.

I liked visiting the fire station. My Uncle Ernie is a great firefighter.

Skill In the first paragraph all the sentences are about one topic—Uncle Ernie. Look for a sentence in the paragraph that tells the most important idea about Uncle Ernie. The other sentences give details about the main idea.

Skill This paragraph is also about Uncle Ernie. What is the most important idea here?

Fire Fighter!

by Angela Royston

How hard is a firefighter's job?

It is busy at the fire station even when there is no fire. Liz is checking the hoses. She wants to make sure they screw tightly to the truck.

Dan is polishing the fire truck wheels. Anthony is upstairs in the kitchen, looking for a snack. He is always hungry! Suddenly a loud noise makes him jump.

Ring!

Ring!

Ring! It is the fire alarm! Anthony slides down the pole.

THUD!

He lands hard. But the thick rubber pad on the ground cushions his feet.

Liz jumps into her boots and pulls up her fireproof pants. She checks the computer. It shows the fire is at 7 Oak Lane. In the truck Liz grabs the walkie-talkie. "Chief Miller! We're on our way!"

"Right!" says the fire chief.

He has gone ahead in a special fast car. "I'll meet you there."

Liz starts the engine as the firefighters jump in. She flips on the sirens and lights and drives out of the fire house. The truck speeds toward the fire.

Cars and buses stop and wait when they hear the siren coming.

The fire chief calls Liz. "I'm at the fire scene. It's an old house that's been empty for years. But someone saw a young boy playing on the porch this morning. He might be inside the house. Tell Dan and Anthony to get their air tanks ready."

"Okay, Chief," says Liz. "I can see the smoke from here. We'll be there in two minutes."

Liz turns the corner into Oak Lane. Flames cover the top of the house.

The fire is spreading quickly. There's no time to lose! Liz hooks a hose from the truck to the nearest fire hydrant. A pump on the truck pulls water from the hydrant to another hose. Liz and another firefighter point the hose at the flames. "Ready!" calls Liz.

WHOOSH!

They hold on tight as the water shoots out. It comes out of a fire hose hard enough to knock a person down.

188

Anthony and Dan are ready to search the burning building. They have put on their air tanks and face masks. Each tank holds 40 minutes of air. That's not much time!

"The boy's name is Luke," the chief tells them.

"Right," says Anthony. He grabs a hose.

"Let's put the wet stuff on the red stuff!" says Dan.

Dan and Anthony run to the back of the house. The fire is not as bad here. Dan feels the back door. If it is hot, flames could leap out. "It's cold," says Dan. They step inside.

Thick black smoke is everywhere. Anthony shines his flashlight around. "Luke! Luke!" he calls. No one answers.

"I can hear fire upstairs," says Dan.

The fire has damaged the staircase. It could fall down at any time. They climb up the steps very slowly.

Outside, the outriggers are set down on the ground. Outriggers are like legs. They keep the truck steady as the ladder is raised. The ladder goes up like a telescope to the top of the house. A hose runs up the side. The firefighter on the ladder shoots water down on the fire. The flames crackle and hiss. They get smaller, then suddenly jump even higher.

Inside the house, the fire rages. It is hot enough to melt glass. Anthony sprays water on the flames. Fire has made the house weak.

"It could come down any second," says Dan. "We must find Luke."

BOOM! A beam crashes down near them. But their helmets protect their heads. CRASH!

"Quick!" says Anthony. "We're running out of time."

They come to another door. But it will not open. Dan swings his ax at the door. Once. Twice. Three times. "It's jammed!" shouts Dan. The roar of the fire is so loud they can hardly hear. "We'll have to use the electric saw."

Anthony switches on the saw. WHRRR! He cuts a hole in the door big enough to climb through.

"Luke!" calls Dan. "Luke?" But the room is empty.

Suddenly the chief calls. "Get out now! The roof is coming down!"

Dan and Anthony race downstairs. They get out just as the roof falls in. "We didn't find Luke!" yells Dan.

"He's okay," says the chief. "We just found him up the block."

"Whew!" says Dan. "Good news!"

Hours later the flames are out. Anthony sprays water on the parts still glowing red. He is tired and dirty—and very hungry!

Liz winds the hoses back on to the truck. Finally she rests. She is tired too. Back at the station Anthony sits down to eat. "At last!" he says.

Suddenly a loud noise makes him jump. "Dinner will have to wait!" laughs Dan.

Ring! Ring! Ring!

Practice E.D.I.T.H.—Exit Drills in the Home

Do you know what to do if a fire starts in your home? Don't wait until it happens:

- Sit down with your family now.

- Talk about how you would get out of the house.

- Plan at least two ways out of every room.

- Decide where you will all meet once you get outside.

A fire drill now could save lives later!

Think, Talk and Write

Talk About It Firefighter Dan says, "Let's put the wet stuff on the red stuff!" Pretend you are there. Tell everything you hear, smell, and see.

1. Use the pictures below to summarize what you learned. **Summarize**

2. Reread pages 184–185. Write a headline that expresses the main idea on those pages. Then tell three details that you would include in an article with that headline. **Main Idea and Details**

3. The author wrote about an actual fire. How did the order of events the author described help you understand the information? **Text Structure**

Look Back and Write Look back through the selection. Notice the tasks the firefighters must do. How hard do you think a firefighter's job is?

Summarize

 R2.5 Restate facts and details in the text to clarify and organize ideas. **W1.1** Group related ideas and maintain a consistent focus. **LS1.9** Report on a topic with supportive facts and details.

Meet the Author

Angela Royston

Angela Royston writes books about all sorts of things. She has written about animals, plants, ships, trains, trucks, cars, and science. Royston was born in England and studied many different things at school. "I feel able to tackle almost any subject," she says. "I most like to work on books that are fun." She likes to read all she can about something before she writes about it.

Read two more books by Angela Royston.

Life Cycle of a Kangaroo

Strange Plants

Skill Talk

Draw Conclusions

as you read by putting together information from the illustrations and the text. Sometimes in a play directions to actors appear in parentheses. Use these directions to help you read the words as the character would say them.

▶ **Ready to Try It?**
Read "Firefighting Teamwork." Then draw a conclusion using what you know and what you've read.

Social Studies Link

The firefighters in the play use teamwork to get a job done. Make a list of other times teamwork is important.

FIREFIGHTING TEAMWORK

a play by Connie Carpenter

CHARACTERS:

Firefighter Kelly (FF KELLY)

Firefighter Sanchez (FF SANCHEZ)

Firefighter Johnson (FF JOHNSON)

Chief

Three or Four Council Members

Scene: A firehouse.
(One firefighter is sweeping. Another is washing dishes. Another is sleeping.)

196

FF KELLY: *(sweeping)* Boy, is this fire station dirty!

FF SANCHEZ: *(washing dishes)* Yeah, we all have to clean up the mud and dirt we tracked in. That last fire was a mess!

FF KELLY: I think Johnson worked really hard. He had to roll up that hose almost all by himself. That was hard work! He's probably upstairs taking a nap.
(Telephone rings.)

FF KELLY: *(stops sweeping)* I'll get that. *(picks up phone)* Firefighter Kelly here.

CHIEF: *(voice from off stage)* Firefighter Kelly, this is the Chief.

FF KELLY: Yes, Chief. What is it?

CHIEF: We're having an inspection by the city council today. Is everything in shape?

FF KELLY: It will be, Chief. With teamwork we should be able to get things in tip-top shape for the inspection.

CHIEF: Good! I'll bring the council right over.

FF KELLY: Right! Good-by, Chief! *(hangs up phone)* We've got big trouble!

FF SANCHEZ: What? Is it a fire? an accident?

FF KELLY: No! The Chief is bringing over the city council for an inspection.

FF SANCHEZ: Uh-oh! We'd better hurry!

FF KELLY: What about our beds?

FF SANCHEZ: Johnson is up there. Do you think he made them?

FF KELLY: We'd better get up there and check! *(Both firefighters run up the stairs. Firefighter Johnson is lying on a bed, snoring.)*

FF KELLY: *(looks at beds)* Just as I thought! Unmade!

FF SANCHEZ: Johnson, wake up!

FF JOHNSON: What? What is it? *(wakes up and rises)* What's happening?

FF SANCHEZ: *(begins making bed)* We have to hurry. The Chief is bringing the city council over for an inspection.

FF JOHNSON: Inspection! Oh, no! Let's get this place cleaned up. *(begins making bed)*

FF KELLY: I'll get the broom. This place needs sweeping. I'll use the pole. It's faster. *(slides down pole)*

(Fire alarm rings.)

FF JOHNSON: The alarm!

FF SANCHEZ: This cleaning will have to wait. *(Firefighters slide down pole and put on their gear. Firefighter Sanchez checks fireboard for location of fire and turns off alarm.)*

FF SANCHEZ: There! I've turned off the alarm. The fire is at 422 East Jay Street. Let's go! *(Firefighters exit; fire truck siren slowly fades away.)* *(Chief and council members arrive.)*

CHIEF: *(looking around)* This place looks great! Kelly, Johnson, Sanchez? *(Chief looks at fireboard to find out where the firefighters have gone. He turns to council members.)* It looks like they've gone to another fire. Well, that's our fire department. They're hard workers, both in the fire station and in the community.

Reading Across Texts

Each selection told of certain jobs firefighters must do. What did you learn about the jobs? Which job do you think is most important?

Writing Across Texts Write a brief paragraph to explain your answer.

Writing and Conventions

Writing Narrative Nonfiction

Prompt *Fire Fighter!* tells a true story about firefighters putting out a fire. Think about other community workers. Now write a narrative telling how one of those workers performs a job.

Writing Trait

Organize the ideas you put in your narrative.

Student Model

Narrative can begin with a topic sentence telling the main idea.

The pronoun *he* takes the place of *mail carrier*.

Narrative nonfiction tells about something real.

Our Mail Carrier

Our mail carrier is a community worker. He delivers letters and packages. Even if the weather is bad, he delivers the mail. Our mail carrier helps the community. He helps me keep in touch with my grandma.

W1.1 Group related ideas and maintain a consistent focus. **W2.1** Write brief narratives based on their experiences: a. Move through a logical sequence of events. b. Describe the setting, characters, objects, and events in detail. **LC1.3** Identify and correctly use various parts of speech, including nouns and verbs, in writing and speaking.

Grammar Pronouns

A **pronoun** is a word that takes the place of a noun or nouns. The words **he, she, it, we, you,** and **they** are pronouns.

> **Liz** starts the engine.
> **She** flips on the sirens and lights.

She takes the place of the noun **Liz.**

Practice Look at the model. Write the sentences that contain a pronoun. Circle the pronoun in each sentence.

Let's Talk About
Responsibility

LS1.0 Students listen critically and respond appropriately to oral communication. They speak in a manner that guides the listener to understand important ideas by using proper phrasing, pitch, and modulation.

Build Vocabulary

Learn ◎ **Skill Unfamiliar Words** are words you don't know. You can use a dictionary or glossary to help you find the meaning of an unfamiliar word. The words in a dictionary or glossary are listed in alphabetical order. Look at the first letter of the new word. Turn to the section for that letter in the dictionary or glossary. Use the guide words at the top of each page to locate the entry for the word. If there is more than one meaning, decide which meaning fits your sentence.

Practice Read "Safety Solution" on page 205. Write this week's Words to Know on your paper. Add to your list any other unfamiliar words from the passage.

Words to Know	mumbles	shrugs	P.M.
	complain	annoy	signature

On Your Own Reread "Safety Solution." Look again at your list of words. Use a dictionary or your glossary to find the meanings of any words you do not know. Write the meanings of these words. Now choose two words from your list and write a sentence for each word.

G3R1.7 Use a dictionary to learn the meaning and other features of unknown words.

SAFETY SOLUTION

As Jamie and Anton come into the house, Jamie's mom is on the phone. She is saying, "It's just not safe!"

"What's up with your mom?" Anton mumbles. Jamie shrugs. Then Jamie's mom hangs up.

"What's wrong, Mom?" Jamie asks.

"Mrs. Johnson just called. Her little boy was almost hit by a car! On our street!"

"That's terrible," says Anton.

"Yes, cars drive too fast, at all hours. Even as late as 10:00 P.M.!" she says. "I wish there were something we could do besides complain."

Jamie has an idea. But he doesn't want to annoy his mother by talking too much. Finally, he speaks up.

"I have an idea," says Jamie. "We need a stop sign on our corner. Then cars can't race down the street."

"That's a great idea!" says Jamie's mom. "We'll write a petition for a stop sign. We'll ask Mrs. Johnson for her signature. We'll ask other neighbors too."

Jamie's mom gives Jamie a big hug and says, "This just might work!"

Need a Review?
See *Words!*, p. W•14 for more information about dictionary skills.

Ready to Try It?
Read *Carl the Complainer* on pp. 208–225.

Build Comprehension

Learn ◉ **Skill Steps in a Process**

- Telling the steps in a process is telling the order of steps to do something.

- Clue words like *first, next, then*, and *begin* tell you in what order you should do the steps.

- When you follow directions, you are following the steps in a process.

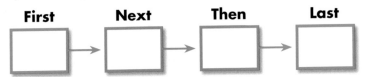

| **First** | **Next** | **Then** | **Last** |

Practice Read "Put It On a Poster" on page 207. Look for clue words that help you see the steps in a process. Think about what the result of each step will look like.

On Your Own **Write to Read** Reread "Put It On a Poster" and make a graphic organizer like the one above. Write each step of the process in one box.

 Need a Review?
See *Picture It!* on p. PI•11 for more information about steps in a process.

 Ready to Try It?
As you read *Carl the Complainer* on pp. 208–225, watch for steps in a process.

R2.5 Restate facts and details in the text to clarify and organize ideas. **G1R2.1** Identify text that uses sequence or other logical order. **G1R2.6** Relate prior knowledge to textual information.

Put It On a Poster

Is there a problem in your school or neighborhood? Do you want to do something about it? One way to help is to talk to people. Let someone know about the problem. If you see a broken swing on the playground, you could tell your teacher.

But what if the problem is a big one? Maybe you want people to recycle instead of making trash. To reach many people at once, you could make a poster. A poster is a big sign. It uses words and pictures to give a message.

To make a poster, you need large paper or board, markers or paint, and a pencil. First, decide on a message for your poster. Then plan your poster with a pencil. That way you can erase if you make a mistake. Next, color or paint over the pencil marks. You can draw or cut out pictures to illustrate your poster. Finally, ask an adult before you hang up the poster.

Skill This paragraph tells how to make a poster. Read all of the steps before you start the process.

Skill Look for clue words that help you see the steps in a process. Think about how the poster would look after each step.

Responsibility

207

Genre

Realistic fiction tells stories about made-up events that could happen.

Carl the Complainer

Written by Michelle Knudsen
Illustrated by Maryann Cocca-Leffler

What does Carl do to solve the problem?

My friends say I complain a lot. They even call me Carl the Complainer.

But hey, some things are just so annoying!

Like TV jingles that get stuck in your head. And paper cuts.

It's five o'clock—the time the town park closes.

"Five P.M. is way too early for the park to close," I complain for about the millionth time.

We turn down Dale's street. "At least we've got a town park," he goes on. "Look —"

"I know, I know," I say, laughing. "Look on the bright side!"

Dale starts laughing.

"Keep it down out there!" Dale's next-door neighbor yells.

"Sorry, Mr. Henry," we both call out.

We go into Dale's house.

BUY SUPER CRUNCH CEREAL!

Sign our petition to save
POWER FRIENDS!

CLICK HERE TO PLAY THE BEST GAME IN THE ENTIRE UNIVERSE!

Get your parents to buy you this! And this!

You could be a space monster on the next
ALIEN TURES!

I show Dale a cool Web site. But an ad pops up—then four more. "Pop-up ads are so annoying," I complain. I start clicking them all closed.

"Wait!" says Dale. "There's a petition to save "Power Friends"! I want to sign it. I love that show."

"Why bother?" I say. "The best shows always get cancelled. It's so annoying."

"That's what the petition is about," Dale explains. "If the network sees that lots of kids like the show, they might keep it on."

"Can anyone start a petition?"

Dale shrugs. "Sure, I guess. Why?"

"Maybe *we* should start one," I say. "A petition to keep the park open later!"

"Great idea!" Dale says. "But how do we do it?"

"There's always the Internet," says Dale.

A few clicks later, we find a how-to site about petitions.

Perfect Petition Pointers

1. Give it a title (for example, "Petition to Make Bigfoot the New School Mascot").

2. Say whom it is addressed to.

3. Say who is sending it.

4. Say what you want to do or undo.

5. Get people to sign it—the more people, the better!

6. Give it to a person or group who has the power to do what you want to get done.

A petition is a written request. People sign a petition to show that they agree with the request. Many petitions are on the Internet, and some are passed around by hand.

Dale and I write up the petition and make copies. Then we get our friends together and tell them about our plan.

"I'll help collect signatures," says Laura.

"Me too!" adds Tony. "It would be great if the park stayed open later."

Mary and Pete want to help also!

Petition to Change Park Hours

To: Hanford Town Council

We, the following community members of Hanford, would like the town park to stay open later. We feel the kids of Hanford need a good place to play baseball (and other things). Grown-ups could stay in the park later, too.

People have been writing petitions for thousands of years. Scientists have even found petitions in the tombs of ancient Egyptians.

We all take copies and split up into teams.

My parents are happy to sign. "That's two names already," I say. "This will be a snap!"

But Mrs. Monroe next door says, "Sorry, kids, now isn't a good time."

At the next house, Mr. Adams listens to about one sentence. "Not interested," he mumbles.

"Maybe we should try some place with more people," I suggest.

We try the train station.

We try the supermarket.

But most people are too busy to even listen to what we have to say.

We all meet up at Dale's. Everybody has been unlucky. "This is so annoying," I groan.

"There must be more people who want the park open later," says Laura.

"That's it!" I shout. "We should be talking to people at the park!"

"Yesssss!" everybody yells.

We sit around Dale's kitchen table and start brainstorming.

"I'll bring treats to give away," says Tony. "People will come for the treats, and then we'll tell them about the petition!"

"We'll need signs too," Mary chimes in.

We set up in the park early Saturday morning. The signs look great. Lots of people stop at the tables. They take treats. And most of them sign the petition!

217

By six o'clock we have ninety-nine signatures.

"If we could just get one more, we'd have an even hundred," I say. "Who haven't we asked?"

"There's always Mr. Henry," says Dale. "But—"

"Good thinking!" I tell him. "Let's go!"

"But—" Dale repeats.

I lead the way to Mr. Henry's house.

Dale gulps and presses the bell. Mr. Henry opens the door.

"Uh, hi," Dale starts. "We were wondering if maybe you would sign our petition to keep the park open later."

Every American has the right to petition the government. This right is guaranteed by the First Amendment to the Constitution!

"The park hours are just fine," Mr. Henry growls. He starts to close the door.

"Wait!" I call out.

"Mr. Henry, you're always complaining that we make too much noise. So maybe you should help us do something about it!"

"Oh, really? Like what?" he snaps.

"You could sign our petition!" I reply. "If the park's open later, we can stay there instead of playing in the street."

Just when I'm ready to give up, Mr. Henry smiles. "You actually have a point there, son," he says. "Tell you what. I'll sign your petition. I'll even get some folks in my writing group to sign it too."

"You're a writer?" I ask.

"Sure. That's why I need quiet."

We end up with 108 names. "I hope that's enough," I say. "The meeting is tomorrow!"

I'm very nervous on the night of the meeting.

Carl's petition is going to the town council, a part of the government. But lots of petitions go to businesses and organizations—from movie studios to sports teams to stores.

The council is sitting in the front of the room.

First, a lady stands up and tells them that dog licenses are too expensive.

Next, a man talks about putting a traffic light on Elm Street.

Then it's my turn.

"Good luck!" whispers Dale.

"My friends and I love the park," I say. "But it closes at five P.M. and that's *way* too early." I hold up

the petition. "All the people who signed this want the park to stay open later."

"I don't know," says the man with the moustache. "Is it a good idea to have kids playing in the park after five?"

"It's better than having them run around in the street," a lady in the audience replies.

That's when I notice Mr. Henry.

"We do play outside in the street when the park closes," I say. "Sometimes the noise bothers our neighbors."

I grin at Mr. Henry. "Keeping the park open later would solve that problem too."

Mr. Henry smiles. But the council members are still disagreeing.

What if they say no?

It's time for the vote. I hold my breath.

"All in favor of keeping the park open until sundown?" asks the lady with the glasses.

One by one, the council members raise their hands.

I can hardly believe it. Our petition worked!

Everybody claps and cheers.

Lots of real-life kids have started petitions. One second-grade class even wrote a petition that made the ladybug the official state insect of Massachusetts!

Dale gives me a high five.

"We did it!" he says. "And the best part is, now you'll have one less thing to complain about."

"Was my complaining really that bad?" I ask.

"Yup," Dale laughs. "It was—"

"I know," I say with a grin. "Really annoying!"

Think, Talk and Write

Talk About It Discuss some reasons why you might want to write a petition.

1. Use the pictures below to help you retell the story. **Retell**

2. What are the steps for creating a petition? **Steps in a Process**

3. Make a flow diagram to show the steps you can take to make an important change in your community. **Graphic Organizers**

Look Back and Write Dale convinces Carl that he should do something to make a change instead of complaining. What does Carl learn about how to be a responsible community member?

Retell

LS1.4 Give and follow three- and four-step oral directions.
LS1.8 Retell stories, including characters, setting, and plot.

Meet the Author and the Illustrator

Michelle Knudsen

Michelle Knudsen says, "I'm a writer, editor, book lover, movie lover, science fiction and fantasy addict, occasional community theater actress, allergy-sufferer, and cat lover, among other things." Ms. Knudsen lives in Brooklyn, New York, with her cat, Cleo.

Read more books by Michelle Knudsen.

Maryann Cocca-Leffler

Maryann Cocca-Leffler has always been drawing and painting. When she was in high school, she painted a mural on the family's garage door! Her first studio was a corner of a basement, but now she lives in New Hampshire where she has a big studio full of light.

Poetry Talk

Humor is what an author or a poet uses to make you laugh—or just smile a little. The first poem is funny because something is in a place where we do not expect it. Another way to make something humorous is to exaggerate.

 Ready to Try It?
Read the Shel Silverstein poems. Look for what makes each poem humorous.

Social Studies Link

Think about the characters in the two poems. Do you think it would be easy or hard to get along with them? Write a short paragraph explaining your answer.

Who's Complaining?

Poems and illustrations by Shel Silverstein

SOUR FACE ANN

Sour Face Ann,
With your chin in your hand,
Haven't you ever been pleased?
You used to complain
That you had no fur coat,
And now you complain of the fleas.

HARD TO PLEASE

(To be said in one breath)

Elaine gives me a pain,
Gill makes me ill,
Winnie's a ninny,
Orin is borin',
Milly is silly,
Rosey is nosy,
Junie is loony,
Gussie is fussy,
Jackie is wacky,
Tommy is balmy,
Mary is scary,
Tammy is clammy,
Abby is crabby,
Patti is batty,
Mazie is lazy,
Tiny is whiney,
Missy is prissy,
Nicky is picky,
Ricky is tricky,
And almost everyone
Makes me sicky.
(Whew!)

Reading Across Texts

Carl, Sour Face Ann, and the narrator of "Hard to Please" all complain. Which of these characters also does something to fix a problem?

Writing Across Texts Write a paragraph telling how the character solved a problem instead of just complaining.

229

Writing and Conventions

Writing Realistic Fiction

Prompt In *Carl the Complainer*, Carl learns how to use local government to make his community a better place to live. Think about your community. Now write a story about what Carl might do to try to improve your community.

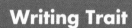

Student Model

Writer uses order words.

The pronoun *he* takes the place of Carl.

Realistic fiction tells about problems that people in real life could have.

Helping the Library

The library needs more books. Carl organizes a book drive. First, he puts up signs so people know about the drive. People from the neighborhood donate books. Next, Carl gets volunteers to work at the drive. They sort the books. The drive is a huge success!

W1.1 Group related ideas and maintain a consistent focus. **W2.1** Write brief narratives based on their experiences: a. Move through a logical sequence of events. b. Describe the setting, characters, objects, and events in detail. **LC1.3** Identify and correctly use various parts of speech, including nouns and verbs, in writing and speaking.

Grammar Pronouns for One and More Than One

He, she, and **it** are pronouns that name only one.
We and **they** are pronouns that name more than one.

> Carl complains a lot.
> **He** writes a petition.

> Carl and his friends want the park to stay open.
> **They** ask people to sign the petition.

He is a pronoun that names one person—Carl.

They is a pronoun that names more than one—Carl and his friends.

Practice Look at the model. Write the pronoun that names more than one.

Let's Talk About
Responsibility

LS1.0 Students listen critically and respond appropriately to oral communication. They speak in a manner that guides the listener to understand important ideas by using proper phrasing, pitch, and modulation.

Responsibility

Build Vocabulary

Learn ⊙ **Skill Suffixes** are word parts that can be added to the ends of words to change their meanings. You can use the meaning of a suffix to help you figure out what a word means. Some common suffixes are *-ly* and *-er, -or.*

When the suffix *-ly* is added to a word, it usually makes the word mean "in a _____ way." For example, *suddenly* means "in a sudden way."

When the suffix *-er* or *-or* is added to verbs it usually makes the word mean "someone who does __." For example, *worker* means "someone who does work" and *actor* means "someone who acts."

Practice Read "Rabbit Tricks" on page 235. Think about the meanings of the words. Also look for any words that end in *-ly, -er,* and *-or.*

Words to Know	treat	chewing	dripping
	practice	wagged	grabbed
	chased		

On Your Own Reread "Rabbit Tricks." On your paper, write all the words you find that have suffixes. Beside each one, write the base word. (That's the word without the suffix.)

R1.9 Know the meaning of simple prefixes and suffixes (e.g., *over-, un-, -ing, -ly*).

Rabbit Tricks

"You can't teach a rabbit to do tricks," said Eric.

"Why not?" asked Lucy. "I'm a good teacher. When Homer does what I want, I'll give him a treat."

Eric looked at Homer, who was chewing on a lettuce leaf. He tossed a ball across the room. "Fetch, Homer," he said. Homer sat perfectly still, the lettuce leaf dripping out of his mouth.

Lucy sighed. "Homer won't do dog tricks. He will learn rabbit tricks. It will just take practice."

A week later, Lucy said, "Eric, see what Homer can do." Lucy held lettuce in front of Homer and asked, "Homer, do you want this?" She moved the leaf up and down. Homer wagged his head up and down. "See? Homer answered!" Lucy said.

"He was just following you," said Eric. He grabbed the lettuce and walked away. Homer chased him.

"See? Now he is playing Follow the Leader," said Lucy.

Eric gave the lettuce to Homer. "Maybe you *can* teach a rabbit to do tricks!"

 Need a Review?
See *Words!*, p. W•6 for more information about suffixes.

Ready to Try It?
Read *Bad Dog, Dodger!* on pp. 238–261.

Responsibility

235

Build Comprehension

Learn ⊙ **Skill Plot and Theme**

- To understand a story's big idea, ask, "What is this story all about? What do the characters learn?"

- You can use something from your own life to understand the big idea, or theme, of a story.

- Plot is what happens at the beginning, middle, and end of a story. Character actions are part of the plot.

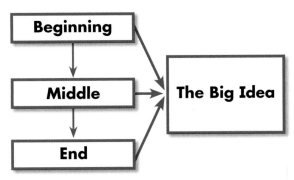

Practice Read "Trouble at the Table" on page 237. Think about what Sara is doing and what lesson Sara learns.

On Your Own **Write to Read** Reread "Trouble at the Table" and fill in a graphic organizer with important plot events and the big idea. Now write about a time you kept doing something when you knew you should stop.

 Need a Review?
See *Picture It!* on pp. PI•12–PI•13 for more information about plot and theme.

 Ready to Try It?
As you read *Bad Dog, Dodger!* on pp. 238–252, watch for important plot events and the big idea of the story.

 G1R3.1 Identify and describe the story's beginning, middle, and ending. **G3R2.2** Ask questions and support answers by connecting prior knowledge with literal information found in, and inferred from, the text. **G3R3.4** Determine the underlying theme or author's message in fiction and nonfiction text.

Trouble at the Table

Victor set the table for his mom, his sister Sara, and himself for dinner. He did not like this job.

Dinner was ready. Sara ran into the room and sat in the wrong chair.

"That's my chair," Victor said.

She moved to the next chair. "That's Mom's chair," he said.

Sara sat in her own chair. She put her napkin on her head. Mom raised her eyebrows. Victor sighed. Sara put her napkin on her lap.

Mom put salad on the plates. Sara used a spoon to pick up salad. Most of the lettuce fell.

"Why don't you use your fork like we do?" Victor asked.

"I am special. I didn't have to set the table," Sara told him.

Sara ate her pudding with a fork. Mom said, "Sara, you know better than that."

Finally, Mom had had enough. "Sara," she said, "tomorrow night you will set the table." Sara sighed. Victor smiled. Mom always says stop while you're ahead.

Skill Think about what Sara is doing. Her actions are part of the plot. You could add them to your graphic organizer.

Skill Perhaps you can use your own experience to help you understand what is happening here. Has a character learned a lesson?

Responsiblity

237

Bad Dog, Dodger!

by Barbara Abercrombie • illustrated by Laura Ovresat

Genre

Realistic fiction means a story is possible. Look for things that could really happen to a boy and his dog.

Do the things that Dodger
does make him a bad dog?

239

Sam wanted a dog.

"If you're a good boy," said his father.

"When you can take care of it yourself," said his mother.

Sam cleaned up his room. He ate carrots and broccoli. He stopped making monster noises at night to scare Molly, his older sister. He hung up his cap after baseball practice.

On the morning of his ninth birthday, Sam found a large box waiting for him. Inside was a puppy. He was black and soft and had big feet. Sam named him Dodger.

The whole family loved Dodger. Dodger licked their faces and curled up on their laps. He nibbled their shoelaces.

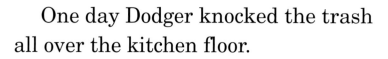

One day Dodger knocked the trash
all over the kitchen floor.

"Bad dog, Dodger!" said Sam.

Dodger wagged his tail and wanted
to play, but Sam was already late for
baseball practice.

242

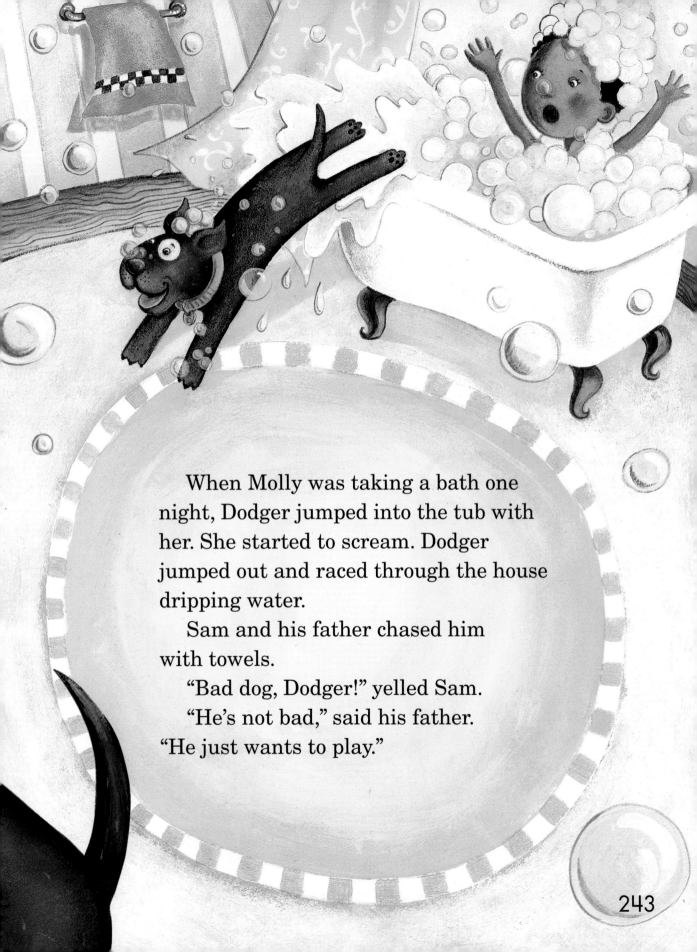

When Molly was taking a bath one night, Dodger jumped into the tub with her. She started to scream. Dodger jumped out and raced through the house dripping water.

Sam and his father chased him with towels.

"Bad dog, Dodger!" yelled Sam.

"He's not bad," said his father. "He just wants to play."

One morning Sam found Dodger chewing his baseball cap. There was a big hole in it. Sam was so mad he almost cried.

They were eating dinner when Dodger pulled down the living room curtains. He wore them into the kitchen. He looked like a bride.

"I've had it," said Sam's mother. "This dog has to live outside."

The next day Dodger jumped over the fence and followed Sam to school and into his classroom.

He knocked over the hamster cage. He ate the cover off a spelling book. Sam's mother had to leave work to take Dodger home.

Saturday was Sam's first
Little League game. He was
up at bat when Dodger came
flying onto the field.

The umpire yelled, "Time out!"
The other team booed.
The coach yelled, "Get that dog!"

245

Dodger grabbed the bat and ran around the field with it. The umpire and the coach ran after him. Sam had to leave the game to take Dodger home.

"We can't go on like this," said Sam's mother. "Maybe Dodger would be better off with somebody who had more time."

Sam knew his mother was right. Dodger needed more attention.

Sam went out and sat in the doghouse with Dodger. "I love you, Dodger." Dodger's tail thumped up and down. "But you need to practice being a good dog."

Suddenly Sam had an idea.

That night he set his alarm to go off half an hour early.

The family was still asleep when Sam got up
the next morning. In the kitchen he filled his pockets
with dog treats.

"Wake up, Dodger!"

Sam pitched a ball to Dodger. Dodger caught it.
"Good dog, Dodger!"

Sam waved a treat in the air. "Come!"

Dodger pranced around the yard with the ball
in his mouth. "This is training, not a game!" yelled Sam.

Finally Dodger set the ball down at Sam's feet. Sam
gave him a treat and said, "Good dog, Dodger!"

247

"Dodger's in spring training," Sam told his parents at breakfast.

Sam pitched balls to Dodger every morning. "Come, Dodger!" he'd shout, waving a treat when Dodger caught the ball.

"Sit!" And Sam would push Dodger's bottom down to show him what sit meant. "Stay!"

After a month of training, Sam decided Dodger was ready to come to a baseball game.

Dodger sat in the bleachers next to Sam's parents.

In the ninth inning, Sam was up at bat with two strikes and the bases loaded. The score was tied. The pitcher wound up to pitch. Everybody held their breath. Sam gripped the bat and hit a fly ball over the bleachers.

"Foul!" yelled the umpire.

Suddenly a flash of black fur leaped
into the air to catch the ball.

Oh, no, thought Sam as the umpire
called "Time out!" and the game stopped.

"That crazy dog again!" cried the coach.
The other team was laughing. Sam's
mother was shaking her head.

Dodger trotted toward Sam with the ball in his mouth. He dropped it at Sam's feet.

"Good dog," said Sam.

He walked Dodger to the dugout. "Sit." Dodger sat.

All the spectators grew very quiet. The other team stopped laughing.

"Stay," said Sam.

Dodger stayed.

Sam hit the next pitch right over the fence for a home run. He ran to first, second, third base.

As he reached home plate, he called, "Come, Dodger!" and everyone clapped. Even the coach.

After the game, the team had their picture taken. Dodger was in the front row and got to wear Sam's baseball cap.

Think, Talk and Write

Talk About It Sam says, "Bad dog!" Later, Sam says "Good dog!" If Dodger could talk, what would he say about the two sentences?

1. Use the pictures below to help you retell the story. **Retell**

2. What did Sam learn about owning a pet? **Plot and Theme**

3. What do you know or what have you read about training a pet? How did that help you understand Sam and Dodger? **Prior Knowledge**

TEST PRACTICE **Look Back and Write** Look back at the story. Do the things that Dodger does make him a bad dog?

Retell

LS1.8 Retell stories, including characters, setting, and plot.

Meet the Author

Barbara Abercrombie

Barbara Abercrombie began writing stories when she was six years old. She likes to write about pets. "When my children were growing up, we had dogs. Our favorite was a Newfoundland named Jennifer. She looked like a large black bear and was often naughty, but we loved her very much. We let her sleep in our beds with the cats." Ms. Abercrombie has two cats now, Stuart Little and Charlotte Webb. Two of her books are about cats.

Read two more books by Barbara Abercrombie.

Charlie Anderson

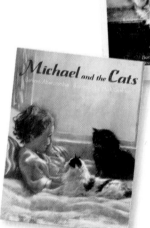

Michael and the Cats

Steps in a Process tell how to make or do something. Notice text features such as numbered steps and photos. These features help explain how to do something.

 Ready to Try It?
Read "How to Train Your Puppy." Watch for numbered steps that tell you what to do.

Science Link

Use the library or the Internet to find out more about training other animals. Make a poster with steps to show how to do it. Tell the class about your poster.

How to Train Your Puppy

by L.B. Coombs

Have you ever tried to make a puppy behave? Training a puppy means making it do the same thing over and over again. You can train a puppy or almost any pet. Here's how.

- Begin training when your puppy is very young.

- Teach your puppy to do only one new thing at a time.

- Pick one word as the command for each new thing you want the puppy to learn, but don't repeat the command too many times.

The words and pictures that follow will help you train your puppy.

First, let your puppy get to know you. Let him sniff your hand. He will learn to know you by your smell.

When you want your puppy to bark, say "Speak." Don't say "Talk" one day and "Bark" the next. Use the same word every time.

Speak!

3 Do not yell at your puppy. This might scare him. Say "No" firmly and in a deep voice. If "No" is the word you want him to remember, use it all the time. Do not say "Stop" or "Don't" when you mean "No."

4 Train your puppy to walk on a leash. Hold your end of the leash loosely. Don't pull your puppy with the leash. Play with your puppy while he is on the leash. It will help him get used to it.

5 After your puppy has done what you ask, tell him he did a good job. Reward him with a treat. Hug and pat your puppy. Training will be fun for both of you.

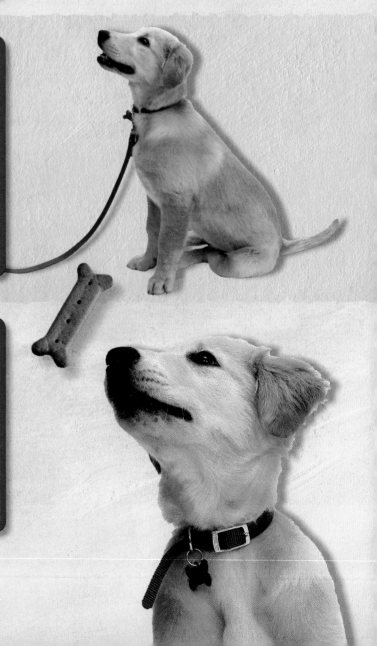

You might want to teach your puppy to sit and stay. When your puppy is standing, gently push his bottom to the ground and say "Sit." After your puppy sits, say "Stay." When your puppy sits and stays for a while, praise him and give him a treat.

Sit!

Stay!

It takes time to train a puppy. But if you choose to do it, this training time can be good for both of you. You and your puppy will build a special friendship.

Reading Across Texts
In *Bad Dog, Dodger!*, which rules from "How to Train Your Puppy" did Sam use?

Writing Across Texts
Choose another rule and write a note to Sam explaining why he should follow this rule with Dodger.

Writing and Conventions

Writing Explanation

Prompt In *Bad Dog, Dodger!*, Sam learns how to train his dog Dodger. Think about the fun Sam has with his dog. Now write a journal entry that Sam might write telling about a new adventure with Dodger.

Writing Trait

Voice shows that a writer knows and cares about a topic.

Student Model

Pronouns *I* and *me* take the place of the name *Sam.*

Realistic fiction tells a made-up story that could really happen.

The writer shows Sam's voice.

> ### Saturday, June 9
>
> I learned something new about Dodger today.
>
> He is a good swimmer! I took him to the beach with me. I threw a stick into the lake. Before I knew it, Dodger swam out to get it. Then he brought it back to me. I can't wait to take Dodger to the beach again!

LC1.2 Recognize and use the correct word order in written sentences.

Grammar Using I and Me

The pronouns **I** and **me** take the place of your name. Use **I** as the subject of a sentence. Use **me** after an action verb. Always write **I** with an uppercase letter. When you talk about yourself and another person, name yourself last.

> **I** read a story about a funny dog.
> The story made Al and **me** laugh.

Practice Look at the model. Write the pronouns that take the place of the writer's name.

Let's Talk About
Responsibility

FOOD
DRIVE

LS1.0 Students listen critically and respond appropriately to oral communication. They speak in a manner that guides the listener to understand important ideas by using proper phrasing, pitch, and modulation.

Responsibility

Build Vocabulary

Learn ⊙ **Skill Unfamiliar Words** are words you don't know. You can use a dictionary or glossary to find the meaning of an unfamiliar word. The words in a dictionary or glossary are listed in alphabetical order. Look at the first letter of the new word. Turn to that section in the dictionary or glossary. Use the guide words at the top of each page to help you locate the word. If there is more than one meaning, decide which meaning fits your sentence.

Practice Read "Boris and Cloris" on page 263. As you read, make a list of the words you don't know. Then use your glossary or a dictionary to find the meanings. Remember, the words will be in alphabetical order.

Words to Know	adventure	wondered	exploring
	climbed	clubhouse	greatest
	truest		

On Your Own Read "Boris and Cloris" again. The story probably makes more sense now that you know the meanings of the new words. Try using the new words in sentences of your own. Write about a friend. Use words from the Words to Know list.

G3R1.7 Use a dictionary to learn the meaning and other features of unknown words.

Boris and Cloris

Boris was bored. All he did was eat and scamper across the floor. Boris longed for adventure.

At the far end of the backyard was a small building. Boris wondered what was in it. He asked Cloris to go exploring with him, but she refused. So Boris went alone.

When he got to the building, Boris climbed through a hole. Two girls were sitting, talking.

"Who can use our clubhouse?" asked one.

"Only the greatest and the truest of our friends," said the other girl. "But, look! There's a mouse in our clubhouse!"

The two girls jumped up and tried to catch Boris. He raced for the hole, but where was it? "Over here," Cloris squeaked. Boris jumped through the hole, and they dashed away.

When they were safe at home, Boris said, "Thank you, Cloris. You are the greatest and truest friend." And he never longed for adventure again.

Need a Review?
See *Words!*, p. W•14 for more information about using a dictionary to find the meanings of unfamiliar words.

Ready to Try It?
Read *Horace and Morris but mostly Dolores* on pp. 266–283.

Responsibility

263

Build Comprehension

Learn   ◉ **Skill Author's Purpose**

The author's purpose is why the author writes. An author may want to:

- share important information.
- explain or describe something.
- entertain readers with an interesting story.
- express feelings or ideas.

Before you read a story or article, ask yourself, "Why might the author have written this?"

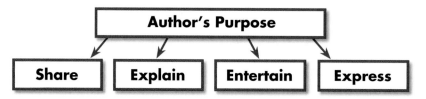

Author's Purpose			
Share	Explain	Entertain	Express

Practice   Read "Tree Houses for Everyone" on page 265. Think about why the author wrote the article. Use the chart above to help you.

On Your Own   **Write to Read** Reread "Tree Houses for Everyone." Write two possible reasons the author may have had for choosing this topic.

⏸ Need a Review?
See *Picture It!* on p. PI•2 for more information about author's purpose.

▶ Ready to Try It?
As you read *Horace and Morris but mostly Dolores* on pp. 266–283, think about why the author might have written this story.

264   **R2.3** Use knowledge of the author's purpose(s) to comprehend informational text. **R2.4** Ask clarifying questions about essential textual elements of exposition (e.g., why, what if, how).

Tree Houses for Everyone

A tree house is a great place to play. People like being in tree houses because they are up so high. Leaves and branches are all around. You can listen to birds and smell fresh air.

In 1997, two men in Vermont named Bill Allen and Phil Trabulsy decided to build a tree house. They wanted to make it a place that all the people nearby could use.

Most tree houses have ladders for climbing up. But Allen and Trabulsy thought about people who use wheelchairs to get around. They can't climb a ladder. Allen and Trabulsy had an idea. They made a ramp instead of a ladder. People in wheelchairs used the ramp to get in the tree house.

Since that time, Allen and Trabulsy have made many tree houses. Each one is made so all people can use it. Their dream is to build one tree house in every state.

Skill Here the author gives the names of two people. Why do you think the author includes this information?

Skill Now that you have read the article, ask yourself, "What idea did the author want me to learn?"

Responsibility

Horace and Morris

Genre

Fantasies are make-believe stories because they couldn't really happen. What makes this story a fantasy?

but mostly Dolores

by James Howe

illustrated by Amy Walrod

Will Horace, Morris, and Dolores remain very good friends?

Horace and Morris but mostly Dolores
loved adventure. They sailed the seven sewers.

They climbed Mount Ever-Rust. They dared to go where no mouse had gone before.

Horace and Morris but mostly Dolores never said,
"This is something we shouldn't do."

They said, "This is something we've got to do!"
And so there was almost nothing they didn't do.

Horace and Morris and Dolores were friends—the greatest of friends, the truest of friends, the now-and-forever-I'm-yours sort of friends. And then one day . . . Horace and Morris had a decision to make.

They didn't want to do anything without Dolores, but as Horace pointed out, "A boy mouse must do what a boy mouse must do."

"Bet you can't say *that* three times real fast," Dolores said with a smile.

Horace and Morris didn't even try. They didn't even smile.
"Good-bye, Dolores," they said.

What kind of place doesn't allow girls? Dolores wondered
as she watched her friends step through the door of the
Mega-Mice clubhouse.

Downhearted, Dolores went on her way—alone. It wasn't long before . . . Dolores had a decision to make.

She didn't really want to do anything without Horace and Morris, but she figured a girl mouse must do what a girl mouse must do. (She said this aloud three times real fast just to prove that she could.)

A GIRL MOUSE MUST DO WHAT A GIRL MOUSE MUST DO.

I'll bet Horace and Morris couldn't do that, she thought. But she wasn't smiling as she stepped through the door of the Cheese Puffs clubhouse.

Day after day, Dolores went to the Cheese Puffs. Day after day, Horace and Morris went to Mega-Mice.

They missed playing with each other, but as they said . . . "A girl mouse must do what a girl mouse must do."
"A boy mouse must do what a boy mouse must do."

Horace and Morris and even Dolores were sure their friendship would never be the same. But then one day . . . Dolores made a different decision.

275

"I'm bored," she announced.

The other girls stared.

"Anybody here want to build a fort? How about a Roque-fort?"

The other girls booed.

"Okay, forget the cheese. I'm sick of making things out of cheese anyway. Let's go exploring."

The other girls gasped.

"Phooey!" said Dolores. "I quit!"

"If you quit, then I quit too!" a small voice said from the back of the room.

Outside Dolores introduced herself. "I'm Dolores."
"I'm Chloris," said the girl.

"Now where can we go to have some *real* fun around here?" Dolores thought and thought. "I've got it!" she said at last.

279

The five friends spent the rest of the day
exploring, Chloris and Boris and Horace and
Morris . . . but mostly Dolores . . .

And the next day they built a clubhouse of their own.

Think, Talk and Write

Talk About It Imagine that you are Horace or Morris or Dolores. Tell how things changed for you in this story.

1. Use the pictures below to help you retell the story. **Retell**

2. This is a funny, entertaining story. What other message do you think the author might be trying to give you? **Author's Purpose**

3. Did anything in the story confuse you? What questions did you ask yourself as you read? **Ask Questions**

TEST PRACTICE

Look Back and Write Look back at the story. What do Horace, Morris, and Dolores do to remain very good friends?

Retell

284 **LS1.8** Retell stories, including characters, setting, and plot. **G3R2.2** Ask questions and support answers by connecting prior knowledge with literal information found in, and inferred from, the text.

Meet the Author and the Illustrator

James Howe

James Howe began writing stories and plays when he was a boy. Mr. Howe has written more than 70 books about funny characters, including Bunnicula and Pinky and Rex. He thinks that the best way to be a good writer is to read—and write, write, write!

Horace and Morris Join the Chorus (but what about Dolores?)

Amy Walrod

Amy Walrod's first picture book was *Horace and Morris but Mostly Dolores.* Ms. Walrod collects toys, lunch boxes, cupcake ornaments, sparkly things, and stuff she finds on the ground. Can you find any of the things she likes to collect in her pictures?

Read two more books by James Howe or illustrated by Amy Walrod.

The Little Red Hen (Makes a Pizza)

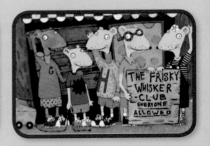

Skill Talk

Main Ideas are the most important ideas about the topic. Sometimes a main idea can be found near the beginning or end of a paragraph. The other sentences in the paragraph give details about the main idea.

 Ready to Try It?
Read "Good Kicking." Also look at the photos and captions. Then look for a sentence in each paragraph that tells the most important idea of that paragraph. This is the main idea.

Social Studies Link

This article says that soccer is a fast-growing sport. Ask the adults in your family what sports were popular when they were growing up. Write what you learn and tell your class about it.

286

Good Kicking

by Rich Richardson
Staff Writer

From spring to fall, you can hear the whoops and hollers of happy children. What's happening? They are playing one of the fastest growing sports around—soccer!

Soccer is played in almost every country in the world. Boys and girls of all ages love this fast-moving sport. Soccer is played in schools and parks across America. Some towns have put together teams of children that play each other.

The small towns around Chicago have some of the best young soccer players. Some children begin playing on teams when they are as young as four or five.

These players chase down the ball.

Good kicking means good footwork.

287

"We want everyone to have fun," says Coach Kay of the Goalers, a team of seven-year-olds. "We have a mixed team of boys and girls. They learn to play together as they learn the rules of the game. Most importantly, they learn what it means to be a part of a team."

Trident players chase down the ball for their team.

Anyone who has ever played a team sport knows that each team member is important. Team members have a responsibility to do the best job they can. If each team member does his or her job right, the team has fun and everybody wins.

"It's always nice to win," Coach Kay states.

Two members of the Scooters congratulate each other.

Coach Kay and members of the Goalers relax before a game. "Being part of a team is more than just winning," Coach Kay says.

"But it's also important that children have fun. Being part of a team is more than just winning. It's learning your role as a team member and knowing your responsibility to your fellow teammates. If we all work together, everybody wins."

Coach Kay should know. Her team, the Goalers, has not lost a game all season. The laughter and smiles on the children's faces also show that they have fun.

Reading Across Texts
Do you think Dolores would have liked playing soccer for the Goalers and Coach Kay?

Writing Across Texts
Write a paragraph telling why you feel as you do.

Writing and Conventions

Writing Animal Fantasy

Prompt The animal characters in *Horace and Morris but mostly Dolores* are really good friends. Think about other animal characters you would like to write about. Now write a fantasy about an adventure these friends have together.

Student Model

Quotation marks are a writing convention.

In a fantasy, animals can do impossible things.

Pronouns are used in different places in a sentence.

Victor and Vera

"What should we do today?" asked Victor.

"Let's sail across the ocean," Vera said to him.

The two rats built a boat out of a plastic bottle. They put it in a puddle.

Then the boat carried them away.

LC1.5 Use quotation marks correctly. **LC1.3** Identify and correctly use various parts of speech, including nouns and verbs, in writing and speaking.

Grammar Different Kinds of Pronouns

The pronouns **I, he, she, we,** and **they** are used as subjects of sentences. The pronouns **me, him, her, us,** and **them** are used after action verbs. The pronouns **you** and **it** can be used anywhere in a sentence.

> Dolores loved adventure. **She** went where no mouse had gone before. There stood Mount Ever-Rust. Dolores climbed **it** quickly.

The pronoun **she** is the subject of the sentence. The pronoun **it** is used after the action verb *climbed*.

Practice Look at the model. Write the pronouns that are used as subjects. Then write the pronouns used after an action verb.

Let's Talk About
Responsibility

LS1.0 Students listen critically and respond appropriately to oral communication. They speak in a manner that guides the listener to understand important ideas by using proper phrasing, pitch, and modulation.

Build Vocabulary

Learn ◉ **Skill Compound Words** are long words made up of smaller words. You may be able to use the meanings of the smaller words to find the meaning of a compound word. For example, a *mailbox* is a box in which we put our mail.

Practice Read "Sigmund's Sign" on page 295. Watch for this week's Words to Know. Which words are compound words? Think about the meanings of the two smaller words in each compound. Then put the two meanings together. Does this help you understand the meaning of the compound word?

Words to Know	signmaker	townspeople	afternoon
	blame	important	idea

On Your Own Read "Sigmund's Sign" again. Write all the compound words you find. Then look around your classroom. Do you see a bookshelf? a chalkboard? a classmate? Write four sentences using compound words that name things around you. Then write what each compound word means.

Read Books!

R1.8 Use knowledge of individual words in unknown compound words to predict their meaning.

Sigmund's Sign

Sigmund was a signmaker. Every building in the town had one of Sigmund's signs. The signs told what was sold in the shop (Toys) or who worked in the building (Police) or who lived in the house (The Guntersons). They helped the townspeople find their way around the town.

But Sigmund thought that signs could do much more than that. One afternoon a large sign appeared in the town square. It said, "Don't blame them." People stopped to read the sign. They talked about the sign. They wondered what the sign meant. They thought about their own actions. Had they blamed someone? Had they been unfair?

Sitting in his signmaking shop, Sigmund smiled. He knew that a sign could do more than help people find their way around. A sign could make people think about an important idea.

Sigmund began to paint another large sign.

 Need a Review?
See *Words!*, p. W•9 for more information about compound words.

 Ready to Try It?
Read *The Signmaker's Assistant* on pp. 298–313.

Responsibility

295

Build Comprehension

Learn ◉ **Skill Author's Purpose**

- The author's purpose is why the author writes.

- An author may want to tell a good story or give information.

- Authors may write to express their feelings or to get readers to agree with their opinions.

Some Reasons for Writing
to amuse readers
to explain something
to inform
to express an opinion
to change readers' minds

Practice   Before you read page 297, look at the picture and the title. What do you think the passage will be about? Now read "The Biggest Signs."

On Your Own   **Write to Read** Reread "The Biggest Signs." Did the author have any of the reasons on the list above for writing? Can you think of other reasons the author may have had? Write to explain your answer.

- -

 Need a Review?
See *Picture It!* on p. PI•2 for more information about author's purpose.

 Ready to Try It?
As you read *The Signmaker's Assistant* on pp. 296–313, think about the author's purpose.

R2.3 Use knowledge of the author's purpose(s) to comprehend informational text.
G3W1.1 Create a single paragraph: Include simple supporting facts and details.

The BIGGEST Signs

You've probably seen them next to a road. Or maybe you've seen one on top of a building. They are huge signs that tell you where to shop or what to eat. These have been around for a long time.

Skill The topic of this article is billboards. Ask yourself, "Why did the author write about billboards?" Perhaps the author is writing to give you information.

In the United States, the first billboards were made more than 100 years ago. The first big signs were circus signs. They told people when the circus was coming. The signs had pictures of clowns and other acts.

Soon many companies were using billboards. They also started adding lights to billboards. Now people could see these big signs at night. Many billboards were put up next to highways, because people were driving more.

Skill You have read about billboards from long ago. Why do you think the author includes this information?

Today some billboards have parts that move. Some even have screens that show short movies. Think about billboards that you have seen.

Responsibility

Genre

Humorous fiction is a funny story about imaginary people and events. Look for the funny things that happen in this story.

THE SIGNMAKER's ASSISTANT

by Tedd Arnold

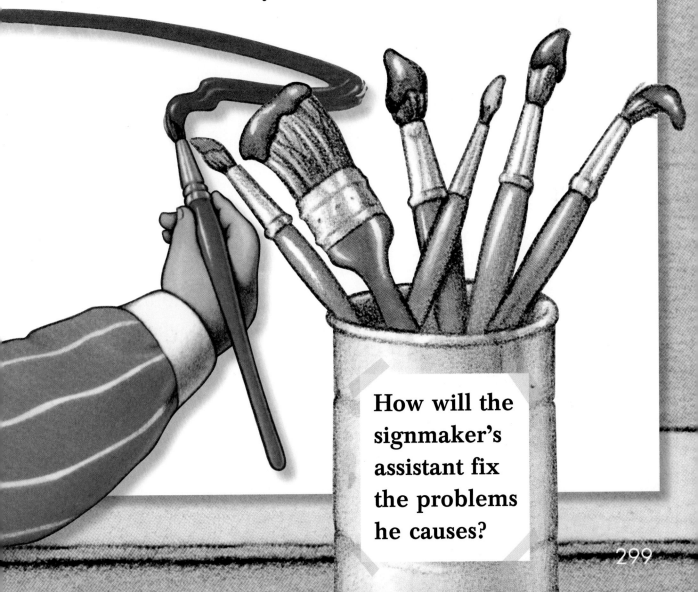

How will the
signmaker's
assistant fix
the problems
he causes?

Everyone in town agreed. The old signmaker did the finest work for miles around. Under his brush, ordinary letters became beautiful words—words of wisdom, words of warning, or words that simply said which door to use.

When he painted STOP, people stopped because the sign looked so important. When he painted PLEASE KEEP OFF THE GRASS, they kept off because the sign was polite and sensible. When he painted

GOOD FOOD, they just naturally
became hungry.

People thanked the signmaker
and paid him well. But the kind
old man never failed to say,
"I couldn't have done it
without Norman's help."

Norman was the signmaker's assistant. Each day after school he cut wood, mixed colors, and painted simple signs.

"Soon I will have a shop of my own," said Norman.

"Perhaps," answered the signmaker, "but not before you clean these brushes."

One day, after his work was done, Norman stood at a window over the sign shop and watched people. They stopped at the STOP sign. They entered at the ENTER sign. They ate under the GOOD FOOD sign.

"They do whatever the signs say!" said Norman to himself. "I wonder. . . ." He crept into the shop while the signmaker napped. With brush and board he painted a sign of his own.

Early the next morning he put up the sign, then ran back to his window to watch.

"No school?" muttered the principal. "How could I forget such a thing?"

"No one informed me," said the teacher.

"Hooray!" cheered the children, and everyone went home.

"This is great!" cried Norman. He looked around town for another idea. "Oh," he said at last, "there is something I have always wanted to do."

The following day Norman jumped from the top of the fountain in the park. As he swam, he thought to himself, *I can do lots of things with signs.* Ideas filled his head.

That afternoon when Norman went to work, the signmaker said, "I must drive to the next town and paint a large sign on a storefront. I'll return tomorrow evening, so please lock up the shop tonight."

As soon as the signmaker was gone, Norman started making signs. He painted for hours and hours and hours.

In the morning people discovered new signs all around town.

Norman watched it all
and laughed until tears came
to his eyes. But soon he saw
people becoming angry.

307

GROCERY MARKET

GARBAGE DUMP

EGGS 29¢

DETOUR

308

"The signmaker is playing tricks," they shouted. "He has made fools of us!"

The teacher tore down the NO SCHOOL TODAY sign. Suddenly people were tearing down all the signs— not just the new ones but every sign the signmaker had ever painted.

Then the real trouble started. Without store signs, shoppers became confused. Without stop signs, drivers didn't know when to stop. Without street signs, firemen became lost.

In the evening when the signmaker returned
from his work in the next town, he knew nothing of
Norman's tricks. An angry crowd of people met him at
the back door of his shop and chased him into
the woods.

As Norman watched, he suddenly realized that
without signs and without the signmaker, the town was
in danger.

"It's all my fault!" cried Norman, but no one
was listening.

Late that night the signmaker returned and saw a light on in his shop. Norman was feverishly painting.

While the town slept and the signmaker watched, Norman put up stop signs, shop signs, street signs, danger signs, and welcome signs; in and out signs, large and small signs, new and beautiful signs. He returned all his presents and cleared away the garbage at the grocery store. It was morning when he finished putting up his last sign for the entire town to see.

Then Norman packed his things and locked up the shop. But as he turned to go, he discovered the signmaker and all the townspeople gathered at the door.

"I know you're angry with me for what I did," said Norman with downcast eyes, "so I'm leaving."

"Oh, we were angry all right!" answered the school principal. "But we were also fools for obeying signs without thinking."

"You told us you are sorry," said the signmaker, "and you fixed your mistakes. So stay and work hard. One day this shop may be yours."

"Perhaps," answered Norman, hugging the old man, "but not before I finish cleaning those brushes."

Think, Talk and Write

Talk About It Suppose Norman asks to come and work in your community. What will you say to him?

1. Use the pictures below to help you retell the story. **Retell**

2. This is a funny, entertaining story. What other message do you think the author might be trying to give you? **Author's Purpose**

3. Think about the signs you see every day. How does this help you know that *The Signmaker's Assistant* is a make-believe story? **Monitor and Clarify**

Look Back and Write Look back at pages 309–312. "It's all my fault!" Norman cried. How will the signmaker's assistant fix the problems he caused?

Retell

LS1.8 Retell stories, including characters, setting, and plot.

Meet the Author

Tedd Arnold

Once Tedd Arnold rode a bus through a town and noticed all the store signs. The signs were nice, and he thought about the person who painted them. The signmaker told people where to go. He controlled what the neighborhood looked like. Mr. Arnold said, "I began to wonder how else a signmaker might have control. Of course, I started thinking of silly signs that could control people and make them do goofy things. That's how the story got started!"

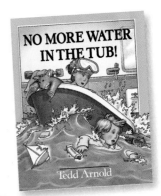

No More Water in the Tub!

Here are two more books written or illustrated by Tedd Arnold.

Tracks

Evaluating Online Sources You can find information quickly on the Internet. You need to know what is good information and what is not. Web sites you can count on often end in *.gov, .edu,* or *.org.* Web sites that end in *.com* may also be useful, but you must check them carefully. The description given with the address can help you choose.

▶ **Ready to Try It?**
Read "Helping Hand." Use the text features such as headings and captions to help you understand what you read.

Social Studies Link

Find out about a volunteer group in your area. Report what you find to classmates.

Helping Hand

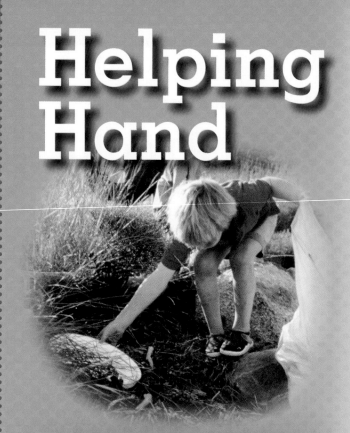

The signmaker learned about being responsible. You can do an Internet search to find out how you can help your neighbors. Use a search engine and type in the keyword *volunteer.* Here are two topics you might find listed. Which one would tell you about volunteer work? To choose, look carefully at both the source and the description.

for more practice

Get Online!

PearsonSuccessNet.com

This is a *.com* Web site. A *.com* site often sells things. It may or may not be a good source.

http://www.url.here

Show Your Colors. T-shirts, bumper stickers, decals, and other items can show your loyalty to a group that you support.

Organizations Started by Kids.
Think you're too young to start your own organization? Hmm . . . maybe you'll change your mind after seeing what these kids have done.

This is a *.org* Web site. A *.org* site is usually a good source.

The link Organizations Started by Kids looks good to you. When you click on it, you get a list of other links. Here are some of them:

Organizations Started by Kids

Care Bags Foundation Annie Wignall, eleven years old

Grandma's Gifts Emily Douglas, nine years old

Kids For A Clean Environment (F.A.C.E.) Melissa Poe, nine years old

Kids Saving the Rain Forest Janine Licare Andrews and Aislin Livingstone, nine years old

Pennies to Protect Police Dogs Stacey Hillman, eleven years old

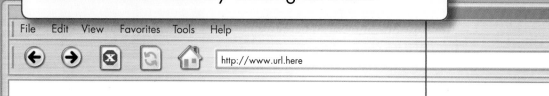

You may want to know more about these volunteer organizations. You decide to explore some of these links by clicking on them.

Kids For A Clean Environment (F.A.C.E.)

Kids F.A.C.E. is an environmental group. Kids from around the world belong to it. It was started in 1989 by nine-year-old Melissa Poe of Nashville, Tennessee. The club provides a way for children to protect nature. The club connects them with other children who share their concerns about environmental issues. Kids F.A.C.E. currently has 300,000 members.

318

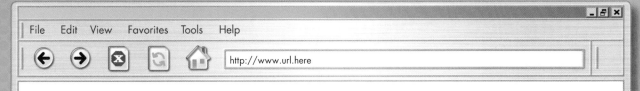

Pennies to Protect Police Dogs

Eleven-year-old Stacey Hillman started Pennies to Protect Police Dogs. She had read about police dogs and their dangerous jobs. One police dog had been shot on the job. The article mentioned that there were bulletproof vests for police dogs, but the vests cost a lot. Over the years, Pennies to Protect Police Dogs has raised more than $100,000. The group has outfitted over 158 K-9 dogs with bulletproof vests.

After reading about both of these groups, you can decide which one might be best for you.

Reading Across Texts

The signmaker's assistant realizes that he has a responsibility to his neighbors. Kid volunteers also help their neighbors. Which group do you think the signmaker's assistant might join?

Writing Across Texts Write a short paragraph explaining how the signmaker's assistant might help his neighbors.

Writing and Conventions

Writing Humorous Fiction

Prompt *The Signmaker's Assistant* is a funny story. Think about funny stories that you have read or heard. Now write a story that will make people laugh.

Student Model

Writer adds funny details.

Contractions combine two words.

Sentences begin different ways.

The Talking Sandwich

Today I was about to take a bite of my sandwich when I heard, "Don't eat me!" I couldn't believe the sandwich was talking to me!

"Don't eat me. You should give me to your sister," said the sandwich.

Then I knew what was happening.

My sister was hiding behind my chair!

W2.1 Write brief narratives based on their experiences: a. Move through a logical sequence of events. b. Describe the setting, characters, objects, and events in detail. **LC1.6** Capitalize all proper nouns, words at the beginning of sentences and greetings, months and days of the week, and titles and initials of people.

Grammar Contractions

A **contraction** is a short way to put two words together. Contractions can combine a pronoun and a verb, such as *will, are,* or *is,* or a verb and the word *not.* An **apostrophe (')** takes the place of one or more letters.

> **I'll** close the shop. *(I + will)*
> Please **don't** leave. *(do + not)*

Practice Look at the model. Write the contractions. Then write the two words used to make each contraction.

Traditions

How are traditions and celebrations important to our lives?

Traditions

Let's Talk About
Traditions

LS1.0 Students listen critically and respond appropriately to oral communication. They speak in a manner that guides the listener to understand important ideas by using proper phrasing, pitch, and modulation.

Build Vocabulary

Learn ⊙ **Skill Homophones** are words that sound the same but have different meanings and spellings. For example, *here* means "at or in this place" and *hear* means "to sense sounds through your ears." These words sound the same but mean different things.

How can you figure out which meaning goes with which spelling of a homophone? Context clues can help you. Remember, context clues are the words and sentences around the confusing word.

Practice Read "Tigers Over Lions" on page 327. Watch for a homophone from this week's Words to Know list. Do you know another word that sounds the same? Write a sentence that uses both homophones.

Words to Know	threw	sailed	field
	bases	plate	cheers

On Your Own Reread "Tigers Over Lions." This time, look for three words that each sound like another word but have different spellings. Write the sentence in which you find each word. Circle the three homophones.

 G3R1.4 Use knowledge of antonyms, synonyms, homophones, and homographs to determine the meanings of words.

Tigers Over Lions

The fifth-place Terryville Tigers played the sixth-place Lincoln Lions last night. The game promised to be an even contest. Tiger pitcher Mike Petrov has won nine games so far. Lions pitcher Kurt Geiger has won 10. Both teams have good hitters. But Petrov had a great night. He threw a perfect game. Geiger was perfect too. Well… almost. For eight and one-half innings, Petrov and Geiger did not give up a hit. Batter after batter went down swinging, popped up, or flied out.

In the bottom of the ninth, the Tigers' last batter was Darrell Swann. He looked at a ball and took two strikes. Then Geiger threw a ball hard and outside, and Swann hit it. The ball sailed into the far corner of right field. Swann raced around the bases. He slid across home plate just before the tag. The umpire yelled, "Safe!" The cheers of the crowd said it all. The Tigers won the game 1–0.

 Need a Review?
See *Words!*, p. W•12 for more information about homophones.

▶ **Ready to Try It?**
Read *Just Like Josh Gibson* on pp. 330–343.

Build Comprehension

Learn **⊙ Skill Compare and Contrast**

- When you compare, you tell how two or more things are alike and different.

- You can also compare and contrast two different authors or two pieces of writing on the same topic.

- Words such as *like, also, but,* and *unlike* are clues that can help you see likenesses and differences.

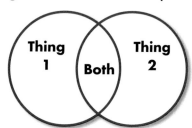

Practice Read "What Makes a Ball Bounce?" on page 329. List clue words that help you see likenesses and differences.

On Your Own **Write to Read** Reread "What Makes a Ball Bounce?" Make a Venn diagram to compare a baseball and a tennis ball. Write one sentence telling how the balls are alike and one telling how they are different.

 Need a Review?
See *Picture It!* on p. PI•5 for more information about comparing and contrasting.

 Ready to Try It?
As you read *Just Like Josh Gibson* on pp. 330–343, watch for comparisons and contrasts.

R3.1 Compare and contrast plots, settings, and characters presented by different authors.

What Makes a Ball Bounce?

A baseball and a tennis ball look almost the same. They are both round. They are about the same size. They both have lines where the parts of the ball come together.

What would happen if you used a tennis ball to play baseball or a baseball to play tennis? The answer is in the bounce.

A tennis ball has much more bounce than a baseball. If you drop a tennis ball and a baseball at the same time, the tennis ball will go higher.

A tennis ball is made of rubber. Rubber helps balls bounce. Baseballs have a little rubber, but not much.

A tennis ball is filled with air. This also helps tennis balls bounce. A baseball is solid inside.

It is a good thing that baseballs don't bounce as high as tennis balls. A baseball hit with a bat can go very far. A tennis ball hit with a bat might bounce right out of the park!

Skill This paragraph tells how baseballs and tennis balls are alike. Did you notice some clue words?

Skill Here is a difference between a baseball and a tennis ball. What other differences can you find?

Traditions

329

Just Like

JOSH GIBSON

by Angela Johnson
illustrated by Beth Peck

 **Genre**

Realistic fiction is made up but could really happen. Look for things that really could have happened to a little girl.

Can a girl really hit a baseball just like Josh Gibson?

Grandmama says there's
nothing like baseball.
The story goes. . . .

Josh Gibson once hit a
baseball in Pittsburgh so hard
that it didn't come down.

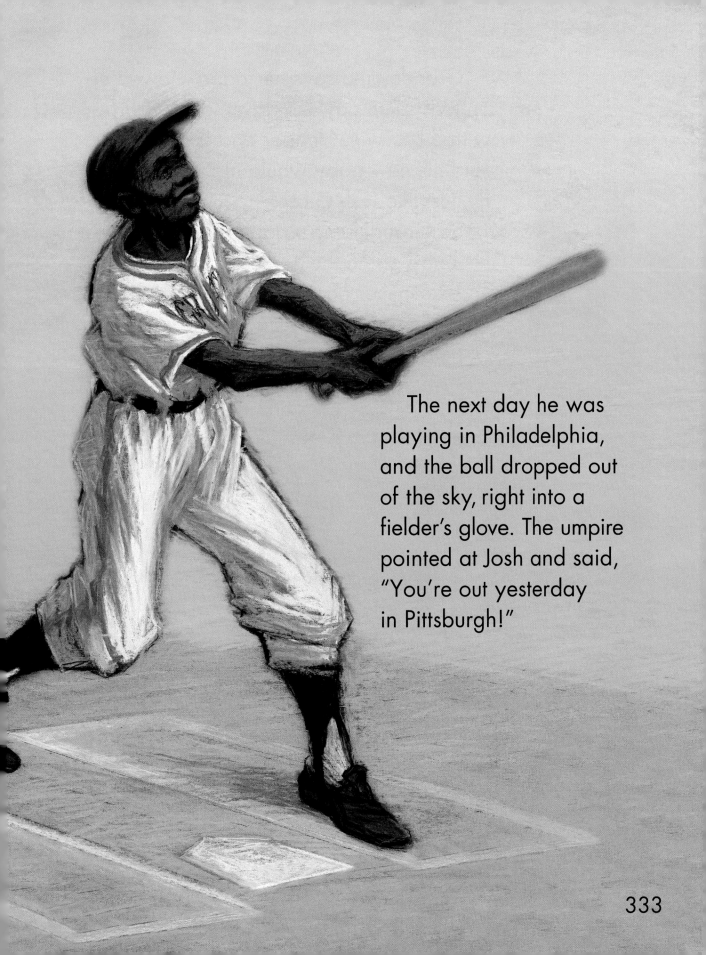

The next day he was playing in Philadelphia, and the ball dropped out of the sky, right into a fielder's glove. The umpire pointed at Josh and said, "You're out yesterday in Pittsburgh!"

Grandmama says her papa showed up
on that same day, the day she was born,
with a Louisville slugger and a smile. He
said his new baby would make baseballs
fly, just like Josh Gibson.

So Grandmama's papa threw balls to
his baby girl in the early morning dew.
Those summer days were like magic as
the balls sailed away, sailed away, gone.

But girls in the forties didn't play baseball. They weren't supposed to take the field with the boys or have batting dreams.

So even when Grandmama got bigger, she still had to stand outside the fence and watch her cousin Danny and the Maple Grove All-Stars batting away.

But every now and again, when the team was just practicing, they'd let Grandmama play too. Then Grandmama would step up to the plate, hit the ball, and watch it soar.

Grandmama says Danny would imagine he was playing with the Dodgers. But she was always Josh Gibson, playing for the Grays, wearing the team colors and hitting away.

Grandmama says she would play all day, with everybody saying she could do it all, hit, throw, and fly round the bases. "But too bad she's a girl. . . ."
Too bad she's a girl. . . .

Until . . . two days,
hot days after the Fourth
of July, Danny hurt his
arm sliding into second,
and there were only
eight All-Stars.

That afternoon the
team looked to
Grandmama—
pink dress with
a white bow, and
Danny's baseball shoes.

And Grandmama
says as she went
to the plate she
remembered . . .

338

baseball has always been
early morning dew and
sunlight, hitting balls with
her papa, and standing
behind the fence,
watching the boys play.

339

The story goes . . .
Grandmama hit the ball a mile
that day, caught anything that
was thrown, and did everything
else—just like Josh Gibson.

341

As she hands the ball to me she says, "There's nothing like baseball, baby, and I couldn't help but love it, especially that one time I got to hear the cheers, hear all the cheers, while stealing home."

Think, Talk and Write

Talk About It A little girl puts on her cousin Danny's shoes and plays baseball. Pretend you are there. Tell about the game.

1. Use the pictures below to help you retell the story. **Retell**

2. Grandmama could not play baseball on the Maple Grove All-Stars because she was a girl. How is that different from girls' sports today? **Compare and Contrast**

3. Look back at page 339 and reread it. What picture did you have in your mind as you read this part? How did visualizing get you more involved in the story? **Visualize**

Look Back and Write Can a girl hit a baseball just like Josh Gibson? Use details from the story to write your answer.

Retell

LS1.8 Retell stories, including characters, setting, and plot.

Meet the Author

Angela Johnson

Angela Johnson has written many great stories. Childhood memories of her father's baseball games inspired *Just Like Josh Gibson*. She says, "I remember the smell of the glove oil, the sound the bats made as the players tapped them on home plate, and the hot dogs I couldn't get enough of. Baseball is a wonderful memory for me. I wanted to write a book about it being a memory for another little girl."

Ms. Johnson recently won an important award to help her continue to write her wonderful stories.

Violet's Music

Do Like Kyla

Read two more books by Angela Johnson.

Text Structures are ways that authors organize information to help readers understand the text.

Sequence is a text structure authors use to show the order in which events happen. Recognizing this text structure can help you remember the important parts of an article.

 Ready to Try It?
Read "How Baseball Began." Watch for dates that tell when important events happened.

Social Studies Link

Look in the library for a biography of Jackie Robinson. Find out why he is an important part of baseball history. Share what you learn with your classmates.

How Baseball Began

by Tammy Terry

illustrated by Clint Hansen

Baseball is called the national pastime of the United States. Hundreds of games are played and watched every spring and summer. But have you ever wondered how baseball began?

Who Invented It?

Well, no one knows for sure who invented the game. Many people believe that a man named Abner Doubleday invented baseball in 1839 in Cooperstown, New York.

Abner Doubleday

In rounders, players threw the ball at runners. If a runner got hit, he was out.

Baseball probably developed from the English game of the 1600s called "rounders."

Settlers living in America played rounders in the 1700s. They also called the game "town ball" and "base ball." Rules of the game varied from place to place. Over the years, the game of rounders became the game we now call baseball. One of the biggest differences between the two games is in how a runner is put out.

In baseball, players tag runners to put them out.

Players and Teams

The first official baseball game was played in Hoboken, New Jersey, on June 19, 1846. The New York Nine beat the Knickerbockers 23–1. More people became fans of the sport as more games were played.

In 1869, the Cincinnati Red Stockings became the first baseball team to get paid to play baseball. They won every game they played that year. Support for baseball continued to grow. More professional teams were formed. In 1876, eight teams joined to form the National League. The American League began in 1900 with eight teams.

YEAR	LEAGUE	TEAMS
1876	National	⚾ ⚾ ⚾ ⚾ ⚾ ⚾ ⚾ ⚾
1900	American	⚾ ⚾ ⚾ ⚾ ⚾ ⚾ ⚾ ⚾

Today, sixteen teams play in the National League. There are fourteen teams in the American League.

YEAR	LEAGUE	TEAMS
2005	National	⚾ ⚾ ⚾ ⚾ ⚾ ⚾ ⚾ ⚾ ⚾ ⚾ ⚾ ⚾ ⚾ ⚾ ⚾ ⚾
2005	American	⚾ ⚾ ⚾ ⚾ ⚾ ⚾ ⚾ ⚾ ⚾ ⚾ ⚾ ⚾ ⚾ ⚾

They play in cities across the United States **(1)** and Canada **(2)**. Each year, millions of people go to baseball games, watch the games on TV, and read about the teams in newspapers. The sport has spread throughout the world, and baseball is now played in countries such as Japan **(3)**, Italy **(4)**, and South Africa **(5)**.

Reading Across Texts

The story *Just Like Josh Gibson* tells that Grandmama played baseball in the 1940s. Use what you read in this article to figure out how long that was after the "invention" of baseball by Abner Doubleday.

Writing Across Texts Make a time line to show the important dates in baseball history. Be sure to include the time when Grandmama played.

Writing and Conventions

Writing Realistic Fiction

Prompt *Just Like Josh Gibson* tells the story of a young girl who admires famous ballplayer Josh Gibson. Think about one of your sports heroes. Now write a story about a character who wants to be like that sports figure.

Writing Trait

Organization builds to a strong conclusion.

Student Model

Being Sweetness

Walter Payton was called "Sweetness." He is Mark's favorite football player. Every day Mark practices hard.

Last Thanksgiving, Mark played football with his brothers. He scored the winning touchdown.

Now his brothers call him "Sweetness."

Realistic fiction has parts that could be real.

Writer capitalized the name of a holiday.

Writer ends with a strong conclusion.

LC1.6 Capitalize all proper nouns, words at the beginning of sentences and greetings, months and days of the week, and titles and initials of people.

Writer's Checklist

✓ Does my writing include parts that could really happen?

✓ Did I include a strong conclusion?

✓ Did I use capital letters correctly?

Grammar Using Capital Letters

Days of the week, months of the year, and holidays begin with capital letters. **Titles** for people begin with capital letters.

I played baseball with **Mr. Gibson** on the **Fourth of July.**

Practice Look at the model. Write your own sentence about something that happened on Valentine's Day. Use capital letters correctly.

Let's Talk About
Traditions

LS1.0 Students listen critically and respond appropriately to oral communication. They speak in a manner that guides the listener to understand important ideas by using proper phrasing, pitch, and modulation.

Build Vocabulary

Learn ◉ **Skill Unfamiliar Words** are words you don't know. Context clues, or the nearby words and sentences, can help you figure out the meanings of these new words. Writers often give examples or an explanation of a word to help you understand what you are reading.

Practice Read "America's Flag" on page 355. Use context clues to find the meanings of this week's Words to Know and any other unfamiliar words. If you need extra help, use a dictionary or your glossary.

Words to Know	nicknames	flag	stars
	stripes	birthday	freedom
	America		

On Your Own Reread "America's Flag." Then write a short paragraph about what the flag means to you. Use at least four words from the Words to Know list.

G3R1.7 Use a dictionary to learn the meaning and other features of unknown words.
G1R2.4 Use context to resolve ambiguities about word and sentence meanings.

AMERICA'S FLAG

The Red, White, and Blue. The Stars and Stripes. These are nicknames for the American flag. You can probably guess why people call the flag by those names. Look at the picture of the flag. What colors do you see? You see red, white, and blue. What patterns do you see? You see stars and stripes.

People hang the flag outside their homes on special holidays like the Fourth of July. That is our country's birthday.

On that day long ago, the American colonies declared their freedom from England. But you don't have to wait for a holiday. You can fly your flag anytime you want. When you look at it, think about what it stands for—America and freedom.

 Need a Review?
See *Words!*, p. W•7 for more information about using context clues to find the meanings of unfamiliar words.

 Ready to Try It?
Read *Red, White, and Blue* on pp. 358–372.

Traditions

Build Comprehension

Learn **⊙ Skill Classify and Categorize**

- *Classify* means to put things that are alike into a group.

- For example, put the following words into two groups: *four, triangle, six, one, square, circle.* Then give each group a label.

- The groups would look like this:

Shapes	Numbers
triangle	four
square	six
circle	one

Practice Read "Flags" on page 357. Find three countries that have red, white, and blue flags. Write the names in a group.

On Your Own **Write to Read** In an organizer like the one above, label the columns "Pictures" and "Colors." Reread "Flags" and look for words for these groups. Write the words in the correct columns.

❙❙ Need a Review?
See *Picture It!* on p. PI•4 for more information about classifying and categorizing.

▷ Ready to Try It?
As you read *Red, White, and Blue* on pp. 360–375, think about how putting things into groups can help you understand what you read.

  G3R1.5 Demonstrate knowledge of levels of specificity among grade-appropriate words and explain the importance of these relations. **G3R2.2** Ask questions and support answers by connecting prior knowledge to information inferred in text.

Flags

A flag is a piece of cloth. But it is much more. A flag is a symbol. It can stand for a country.

A flag sends a message. Each color and picture on a flag tells something. The color red stands for courage. The color white stands for peace. The color blue stands for freedom. The United States flag is red, white, and blue. Many other countries have red, white, and blue flags. The flags of France and Laos are red, white, and blue.

Many flags have pictures. The picture on a flag sends a message. A picture of an eagle might stand for freedom. The flag of Egypt and Ecuador each has an eagle on it. Other flags, like the U.S. flag, have stars. The flag of China has five stars. The flag of Ghana has one big star. The Turkish flag has a star and the shape of the moon.

Skill Start looking for words to add to your "Colors" column. Also notice the names of some countries that have red, white, and blue flags.

Skill This paragraph tells about pictures on flags. What words could you add to your "Pictures" group?

Traditions

357

Red, White, and Blue

The Story of
THE AMERICAN FLAG

BY
John Herman

ILLUSTRATED BY
Shannan Stirnweiss

Genre

Narrative nonfiction gives facts in the form of a story. Look for facts as you read.

How did the American flag change over the years?

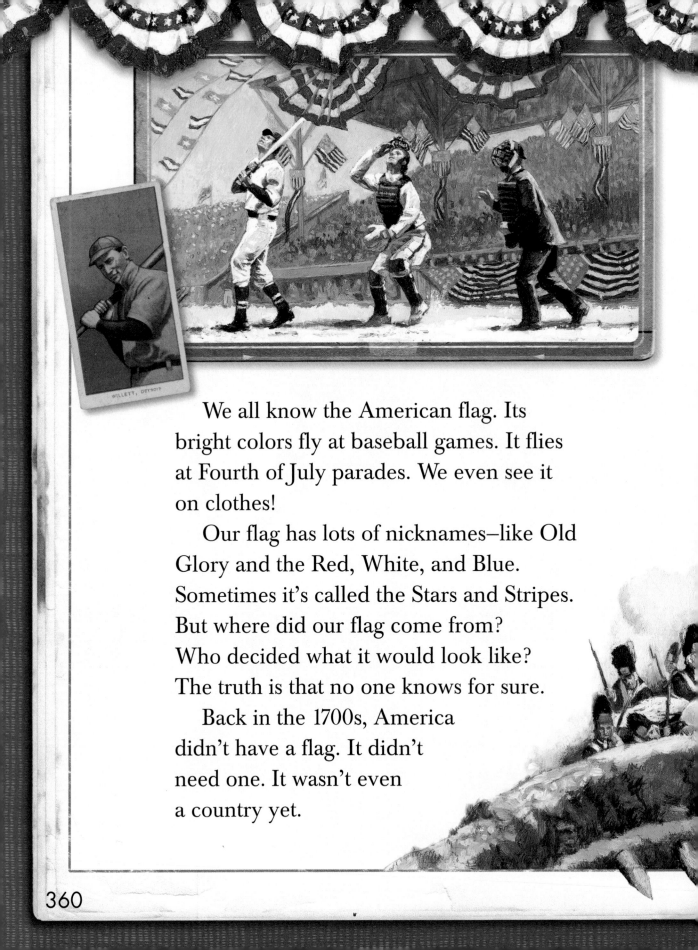

We all know the American flag. Its bright colors fly at baseball games. It flies at Fourth of July parades. We even see it on clothes!

Our flag has lots of nicknames—like Old Glory and the Red, White, and Blue. Sometimes it's called the Stars and Stripes. But where did our flag come from? Who decided what it would look like? The truth is that no one knows for sure.

Back in the 1700s, America didn't have a flag. It didn't need one. It wasn't even a country yet.

It was just thirteen colonies. The colonies belonged to England. The English flag flew in towns from New Hampshire to Georgia.

But as time went on, the thirteen colonies didn't want to belong to England anymore. Americans decided to fight for their freedom.

A war began. It was the American Revolution. Now a new flag was needed—an American flag.

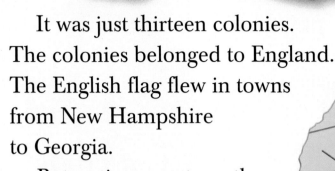

The original 13 American colonies

New Hampshire
Massachusetts
Rhode Island
Connecticut
New York
New Jersey
Pennsylvania
Delaware
Maryland
Virginia
North Carolina
South Carolina
Georgia

Who made our first flag? Some people say it was a woman named Betsy Ross. Maybe you've heard of her. Betsy Ross owned a sewing shop in Philadelphia. She was famous for her sewing.

The story is that one day a general came to see her. The general was George Washington. He was the head of the American army.

General Washington wanted a new flag. It would make his soldiers feel like a real army fighting for a real country.

He wanted Betsy Ross to make this flag. He drew a picture of what he wanted.

Betsy Ross

George Washington

First American flag

Betsy Ross made some changes. Then she showed the picture to General Washington. He liked it!

Betsy Ross sewed the flag. And that was the very first Stars and Stripes.

That is the story—and it's a good one. But is it true? Betsy Ross's grandson said it was. He said that Betsy told him the story when he was a little boy and she was an old woman of eighty-four. But there is no proof for this story. So what do we know *for sure?*

We know that during the Revolution the colonists used lots of different flags.

Flags from the Revolutionary War

But once the colonies became the United States of America, the country needed *one* flag—the same flag for everybody.

So on June 14, 1777, a decision was made. The flag was going to have thirteen red and white stripes. The flag was also going to have thirteen white stars on a blue background, one for each of the thirteen colonies. Now the United States had a flag.

Congress had picked the colors and the stars and stripes. But Congress did not say where the stars and stripes had to go. So the flag still did not always look the same!

People could put them any way they liked. Sometimes the stripes were up and down, like this.

Sometimes the stars were in a circle, like this.

But nobody minded. Up and down or side to side, the stars and stripes still stood for the United States.

Over the years, the flag became more and more important to people.

In 1812, the United States was at war with England again. British soldiers came to America. They sailed up our rivers. They marched down our streets. They even burned down the White House—the home of the President.

Flag from battle at Fort McHenry

On the night of September 13, 1814, British soldiers bombed a fort in Maryland. All that night a man watched the fighting. His name was Francis Scott Key. He was afraid. What if the American soldiers in the fort gave up?

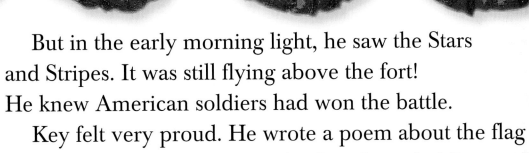

But in the early morning light, he saw the Stars and Stripes. It was still flying above the fort! He knew American soldiers had won the battle.

Key felt very proud. He wrote a poem about the flag on the fort. The poem was "The Star-Spangled Banner." Later the poem was put to music. This song about our flag became a song for our whole country.

Francis Scott Key

The flag that Francis Scott Key saw had fifteen stripes and fifteen stars.

Why? Because by then there were two more states—Vermont and Kentucky.

American flag in 1814

First Fifteen American States

Vermont

Kentucky

New Hampshire
Massachusetts
Rhode Island
Connecticut
New York
New Jersey
Pennsylvania
Delaware
Maryland
Virginia
North Carolina
South Carolina
Georgia

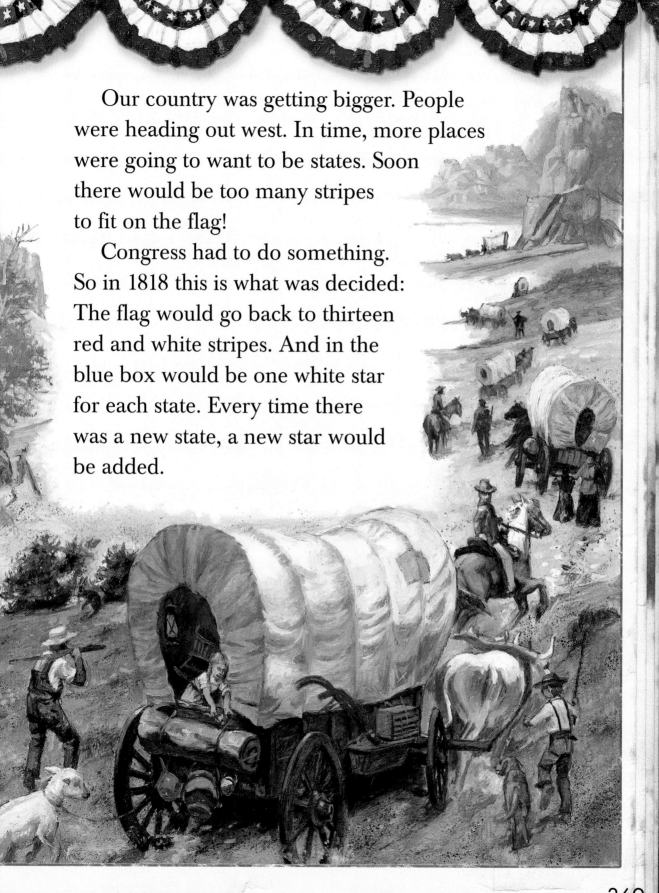

Our country was getting bigger. People were heading out west. In time, more places were going to want to be states. Soon there would be too many stripes to fit on the flag!

Congress had to do something. So in 1818 this is what was decided: The flag would go back to thirteen red and white stripes. And in the blue box would be one white star for each state. Every time there was a new state, a new star would be added.

At last the Stars and Stripes looked the same everywhere it flew. And Americans were proud of their flag. They took the flag with them as they moved west. The flag crossed the Mississippi River and the great grassy plains and the Rocky Mountains. It made it all the way to California.

More and more states were added to the country. And more and more stars were added to the flag. By 1837, there were twenty-six stars on the flag. By 1850, there were thirty-one.

American flag in 1850

The United States in 1850

This map shows all the states as of 1850.

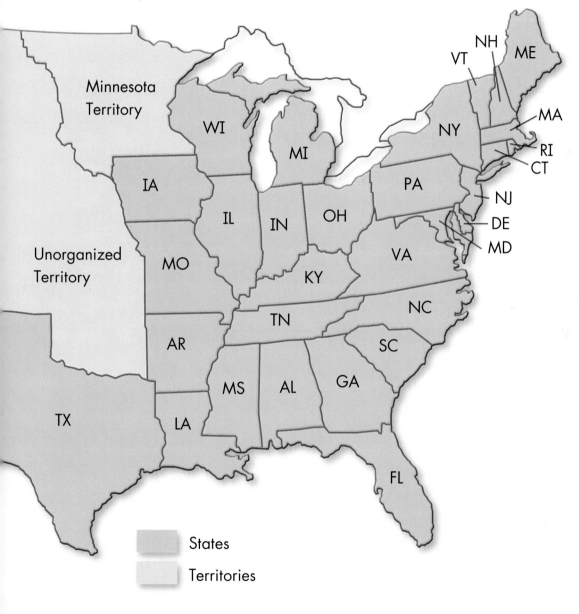

Minnesota Territory

Unorganized Territory

WI
MI
IA
IL
IN
OH
MO
KY
AR
TN
MS
AL
GA
LA
TX
FL
VA
NC
SC
PA
NY
VT
NH
ME
MA
RI
CT
NJ
DE
MD

States
Territories

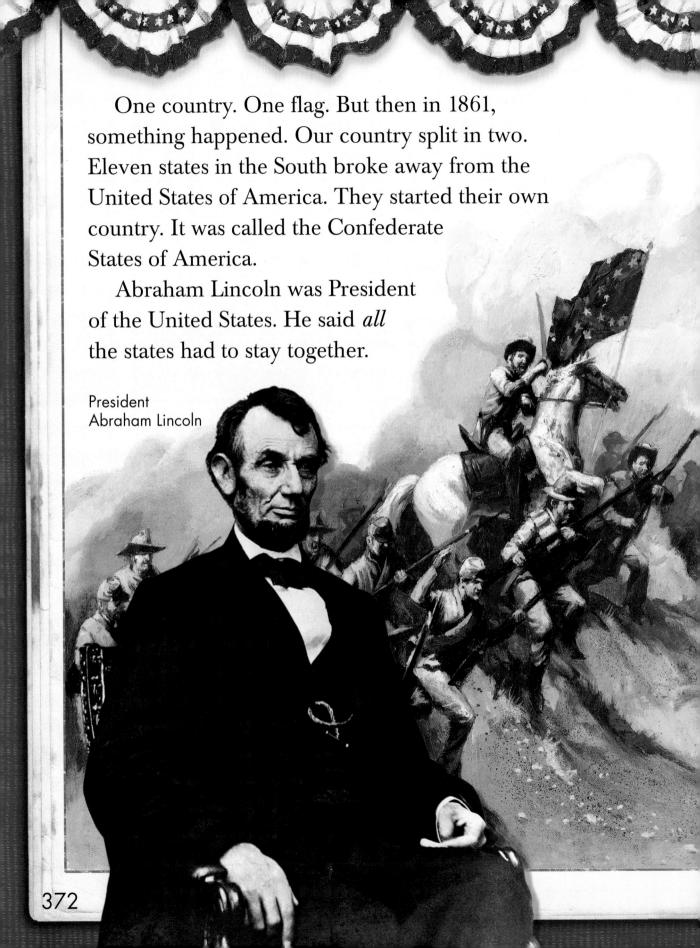

One country. One flag. But then in 1861, something happened. Our country split in two. Eleven states in the South broke away from the United States of America. They started their own country. It was called the Confederate States of America.

Abraham Lincoln was President of the United States. He said *all* the states had to stay together.

President
Abraham Lincoln

War broke out—the Civil War. It was a very sad time in the history of our country.

The eleven southern states stopped flying the Stars and Stripes. They had their own flag.

In the North, some people wanted eleven stars taken off the Stars and Stripes. But Abraham Lincoln would not do that. He said the states would get back together. He was right. The Civil War ended in 1865. The North won. And the United States was one country under one flag again.

On June 14, 1877, the flag had a birthday—a big one. It was 100 years old. All across the country, people had picnics and parties and parades. June 14 became a holiday—Flag Day.

Today our flag has fifty stars for the fifty United States of America. Some flags are huge. One weighs 500 pounds! It is flown every Fourth of July from the George Washington Bridge.

The American flag flies in towns and cities from coast to coast.

And that's not all. In 1969, two American astronauts were the first people ever to land on the moon. The astronauts took lots of moon rocks back to Earth. They also left something on the moon . . . the Stars and Stripes.

And do you know what? Our flag is still flying there!

Think, Talk and Write

Talk About It What did you learn about the flag that you didn't know before? Talk about something that surprised you.

1. Use the pictures below to summarize what you learned. **Summarize**

2. How are the original thirteen states shown on the flag? How are the rest of the states shown? **Classify and Categorize**

3. Did anything in this selection confuse you? Where did you have a problem while reading? What did you do about it? **Monitor and Clarify**

Look Back and Write How has the American flag changed? Use details from the selection in writing your answer.

Summarize

R2.5 Restate facts and details in the text to clarify and organize ideas.
LS1.9 Report on a topic with supportive facts and details.

Meet the Author

John Herman

John Herman grew up near New York City. He knew he wanted to be a writer when he was twelve years old. Now he writes books for adults, teenagers, and children.

Mr. Herman likes to make up stories. *Red, White, and Blue* gave him a chance to write about real events. He loves reading about American history, so this was a new thing for him to try. He hopes to write more books like this in the future!

The Flag We Love
by Pam Muñoz Ryan

Read more books about the American flag.

Betsy Ross
by Alexandra Wallner

Traditions

Poetry Talk

Alliteration and Rhyme are special tools of writers. Songs and poems are often organized in verses with a rhyming pattern. In this song, the first two lines rhyme as do the third and fifth lines. Alliteration is the repetition of beginning sounds of words. Notice how often words beginning with *f* appear.

 Ready to Try It?
As you read "You're a Grand Old Flag," think about how the songwriter feels about the American flag.

Social Studies Link

The flag is called an *emblem.* Use a dictionary to learn the meaning of this word. Make a list of other American emblems.

You're a Grand Old Flag

by George M. Cohan

You're a grand old flag,
You're a high flying flag
And forever in peace may
   you wave.
You're the emblem of the
   land I love.
The home of the free and
   the brave.

Ev'ry heart beats true
'Neath the red, white, and blue,
Where there's never a boast
   or brag.
Should auld acquaintance
   be forgot,
Keep your eye on the grand
   old flag.

Reading Across Texts

"You're a Grand Old Flag" is one song about the flag of the United States. What other song about the flag did you read about in *Red, White, and Blue*?

Writing Across Texts Make a list of other patriotic songs that you know.

Writing and Conventions

Writing Narrative Nonfiction

Prompt *Red, White, and Blue* tells the history of the American flag. Think about other American symbols and traditions. Now write about one of those symbols or traditions.

WILLETT, DETROIT

Writing Trait

Good writers **focus** their **ideas** on one main idea and then give details.

Student Model

The Statue of Liberty

Writer focuses on one main idea.

The Statue of Liberty is an American symbol. The statue is of a woman. She stands for freedom.

Writer uses quotation marks for spoken words.

"Come in and be free," she seems to say.

Narrative nonfiction tells about real things.

The statue is the first thing many new Americans see when they come here.

W2.1 Write brief narratives based on their experiences: a. Move through a logical sequence of events. b. Describe the setting, characters, objects, and events in detail. **LC1.5** Use quotation marks correctly.

Grammar Using Quotation Marks

Quotation marks (" ") show the beginning and the end of the words someone says. The speaker's name and words such as **said** and **asked** are not inside the quotation marks.

"Can you make a flag?" **asked** General Washington.

"I will try," Betsy Ross **said**.

Practice Look at the model. Write two of your own sentences that use quotation marks.

Let's Talk About
Traditions

LS1.0 Students listen critically and respond appropriately to oral communication. They speak in a manner that guides the listener to understand important ideas by using proper phrasing, pitch, and modulation.

Build Vocabulary

Learn ⊙ **Skill Synonyms** are different words that mean the same or almost the same thing. For example, *feel* is a synonym for *touch*. When you are reading and you come to a word you don't know, look for a nearby word you do know that might be a synonym. To see if it will help you understand the meaning of the word you don't know, try the synonym in place of the unknown word. Does it make sense?

Practice Read "Making a Present" on page 385. Look for words that might be synonyms for this week's Words to Know. Also watch for synonyms for other unfamiliar words.

Words to Know	bank	present	favorite
	basket	aunt	collects

On Your Own Reread "Making a Present." Write the vocabulary words in alphabetical order. If you found a synonym in the text for any of the words, write it beside the vocabulary word. Then look up the rest of the words in a dictionary and write their meanings on your list.

R1.7 Understand and explain common antonyms and synonyms. **G3R1.7** Use a dictionary to learn the meaning and other features of unknown words. **G1R2.4** Use context to resolve ambiguities about word and sentence meanings.

Making a Present

Is someone you know having a birthday soon? What gift will you give that person? You do not have to break your piggy bank to buy a present. A gift you make for someone special will show that you care.

It is not difficult or hard to make a present. Ask yourself what the person likes or enjoys. What is his or her favorite color? favorite hobby? favorite food? See if the answers give you an idea.

If you have a garden, you could pick flowers. Find a basket or bowl at home. Arrange the flowers in it. This makes a nice gift for your mother or father.

Make a picture frame out of cardboard. Decorate it. Put a photo in the frame. This is a good present for an aunt or uncle.

Another easy gift to make is a pencil holder. If the person collects, or gathers, their loose pens and pencils, a pencil holder will keep them in one place. Find an old cup or mug. Decorate it. You could even put the person's name on it.

It's easy to make a special present for someone you love.

 Need a Review?
See the *Words!*, p. W•3 for more information about synonyms.

 Ready to Try It?
Read *A Birthday Basket for Tía* on pp. 388–401.

Traditions

Build Comprehension

Learn   **Skill Draw Conclusions**

- When you read, you can draw conclusions or figure out more about the characters and what happens in the story.

- Use what you have read and what you know about real life to ask or answer questions.

- Find words in the text to support your ideas.

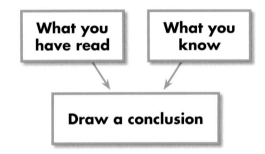

> | What you have read | What you know |
>
> **Draw a conclusion**

Practice   Read "Empty Eggshells" on page 387. Draw conclusions about what you read using what you know about real life.

On Your Own   **Write to Read** Reread "Empty Eggshells." Use a graphic organizer to draw conclusions about Jorge and Danny. Write two sentences about your conclusions.

 Need a Review?
See *Picture It!* on p. PI·7 for more information about drawing conclusions.

 Ready to Try It?
As you read *A Birthday Basket for Tía* on pp. 388–401, draw conclusions to help you understand the text.

R2.5 Restate facts and details in the text to clarify and organize ideas.
G3R2.2 Ask questions and support answers by connecting prior knowledge to information inferred in text.

Empty Eggshells

Jorge asked Danny to come early to his party.

"Help me make cascarones," he said.

What are cascarones? Danny wondered.

When Danny arrived he saw a carton of eggs. But they were just eggshells with a hole at the top—no egg inside.

"What do we do with these?" Danny asked.

"First, we will paint the eggshells. Next, we will fill each egg with tiny bits of paper," Jorge told him. "Then my mother will glue paper over each hole."

Before the party, Jorge's father hid the eggs in the apartment. All the children went on an egg hunt, and all the eggs were found. Then—surprise! Jorge cracked one open over the top of Danny's head! The colored paper rained down! Danny laughed and laughed. Soon everyone at the party was cracking cascarones over one another's heads!

Skill Here you can draw the conclusion that Jorge and Danny are friends. Jorge asked Danny to come early and help.

Skill You might draw the conclusion that when the children crack the eggs on each other's heads, they do not hurt each other.

A Birthday Basket for Tía

by Pat Mora

illustrated by Cecily Lang

Genre

Realistic fiction is a story with characters and events that are like people and events in real life.

What will be in the birthday basket for Tía?

Today is secret day. I curl my cat into my arms and say, "Ssshh, Chica. Can you keep our secret, silly cat?"

Today is special day. Today is my great-aunt's ninetieth birthday. Ten, twenty, thirty, forty, fifty, sixty, seventy, eighty, ninety. Ninety years old. *¡Noventa años!*

At breakfast Mamá asks, "What is today, Cecilia?" I say, "Special day. Birthday day."

Mamá is cooking for the surprise party. I smell beans bubbling on the stove. Mamá is cutting fruit—pineapple, watermelon, mangoes. I sit in the backyard and watch Chica chase butterflies. I hear bees bzzzzz.

I draw pictures in the sand with a stick. I draw a picture of my aunt, my *Tía*. I say, "Chica, what will we give Tía?"

Chica and I walk around the front yard and
the backyard looking for a good present. We walk
around the house. We look in Mamá's room. We look
in my closet and drawers.

I say, "Chica, shall we give her my little pots, my
piggy bank, my tin fish, my dancing puppet?"

I say, "Mamá, can Chica and I use this basket?"

Mamá asks, "Why, Cecilia?"

"It's a surprise for the surprise party," I answer.
Chica jumps into the basket. "No," I say. "Not for
you, silly cat. This is a birthday basket for Tía."

I put a book in the basket. When Tía comes to our house, she reads it to me. It's our favorite book. I sit close to her on the sofa. I smell her perfume. Sometimes Chica tries to read with us. She sits on the book. I say, "Silly cat. Books are not for sitting."

I put Tía's favorite mixing bowl on the book in the basket. Tía and I like to make *bizcochos*, sugary cookies for the family.

Tía says, "Cecilia, help me stir the cookie dough." She says, "Cecilia, help me roll the cookie dough." When we take the warm cookies from the oven, Tía says, "Cecilia, you are a very good cook."

393

I put a flowerpot in the mixing bowl on the book in the basket. Tía and I like to grow flowers for the kitchen window. Chica likes to put her face in the flowers. "Silly cat," I say.

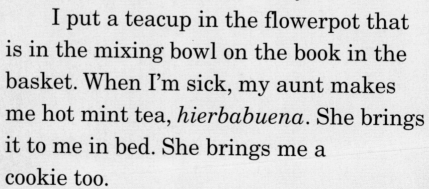

I put a teacup in the flowerpot that is in the mixing bowl on the book in the basket. When I'm sick, my aunt makes me hot mint tea, *hierbabuena*. She brings it to me in bed. She brings me a cookie too.

I put a red ball in the teacup that is in the flowerpot in the mixing bowl on the book in the basket. On warm days Tía sits outside and throws me the ball.

She says, "Cecilia, when I was a little girl in Mexico, my sisters and I played ball. We all wore long dresses and had long braids."

Chica and I go outside. I pick flowers to decorate Tía's basket. On summer days when I am swinging high up to the sky, Tía collects flowers for my room.

Mamá calls, "Cecilia, where are you?"

Chica and I run and hide our surprise.

I say, "Mamá, can you find the birthday basket for Tía?"

Mamá looks under the table. She looks in the refrigerator. She looks under my bed. She asks, "Chica, where is the birthday basket?"

Chica rubs against my closet door. Mamá and I laugh. I show her my surprise.

After my nap, Mamá and I fill a piñata with candy. We fill the living room with balloons. I hum, mmmmm, a little work song like the one Tía hums when she sets the table or makes my bed. I help Mamá set the table with flowers and tiny cakes.

"Here come the musicians," says Mamá. I open the front door. Our family and friends begin to arrive too.

I curl Chica into my arms. Then Mamá says, "Sshh, here comes Tía."

I rush to open the front door. "Tía! Tía!" I shout. She hugs me and says,

"Cecilia, *¿qué pasa?* What is this?"

"SURPRISE!" we all shout. "¡*Feliz cumpleaños!* Happy birthday!" The musicians begin to play their guitars and violins.

"Tía! Tía!" I say, "It's special day, birthday day!
It's your ninetieth birthday surprise party!"
Tía and I laugh.

I give her the birthday basket. Everyone gets close to see what's inside. Slowly Tía smells the flowers. She looks at me and smiles. Then she takes the red ball out of the teacup and the teacup out of the flowerpot.

She pretends to take a sip of tea and we all laugh.

Carefully, Tía takes the flowerpot out of the bowl and the bowl off of the book. She doesn't say a word. She just stops and looks at me. Then she takes our favorite book out of the basket.

And guess who jumps into the basket?

Chica. Everyone laughs.

Then the music starts and my aunt surprises me. She takes my hands in hers. Without her cane, she starts to dance with me.

Think, Talk and Write

Talk About It Pretend you made a birthday basket for someone. What six things would you put in it? Why?

1. Use the pictures below to help you retell the story. **Retell**

2. Think about the things Cecilia put into the basket for Tía. What conclusions can you draw about how Cecilia feels about Tía? **Draw Conclusions**

3. What do you know or what have you read about birthday parties? How did that help you understand the story? **Prior Knowledge**

Look Back and Write Look back at the story. What did Cecilia first think she might give to Tía? What things did Cecilia finally give to Tía? Make two lists. Use details from the selection as you write your answer.

Retell

402

Meet the Author

Pat Mora

Read two more books by Pat Mora.

Though Pat Mora grew up in Texas, she came from a home where both English and Spanish were spoken. When she started writing books, Ms. Mora realized she wanted to write about her experience as a Mexican American. "It was like opening a treasure chest," Ms. Mora says. "My whole Mexican heritage was something I could write about."

Ms. Mora tells students to write about what they love. She says, "The trick is how we bring everything that we are to the page—everything."

This Big Sky

Tomás and the Library Lady

Online Directories

list links to many topics. A link is a special text feature of online text. Links are underlined or appear in a different color. Clicking on a link takes you to another Web site. When you are using an online directory to help you find information, you can click on the link that is closest to what you are looking for.

 Ready to Try It?

Read "Family Traditions: Birthdays." Use the illustrations along with the text to learn how an online directory works.

Social Studies Link

Interview members of your family about family traditions they celebrated.

404

Family Traditions: Birthdays

How can you find out more about birthdays? You can go to an Internet online directory. Here are some of the topics you might find listed there.

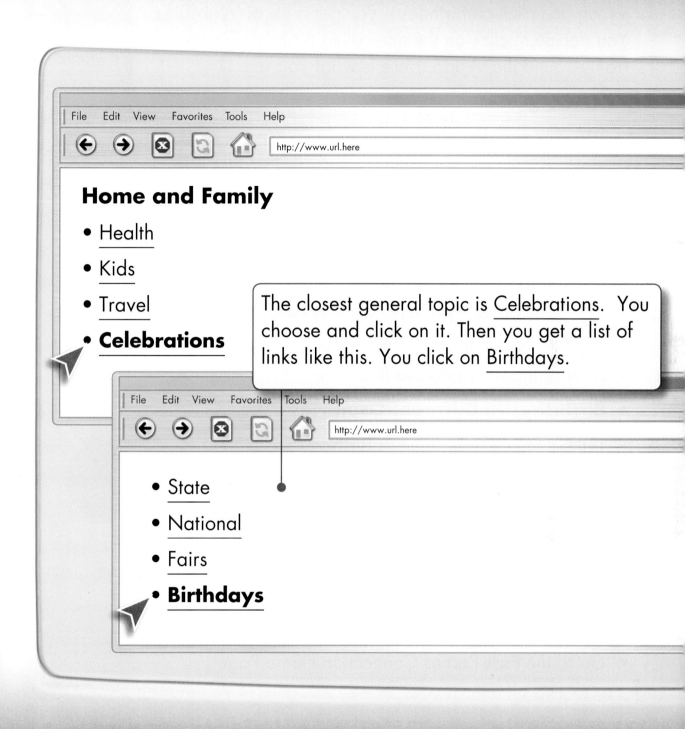

Home and Family

- Health
- Kids
- Travel
- **Celebrations**

The closest general topic is Celebrations. You choose and click on it. Then you get a list of links like this. You click on Birthdays.

- State
- National
- Fairs
- **Birthdays**

When you click on Birthdays, you get a list of Web sites. You decide to click on the one called Birthday Traditions from Around the World. Here is what you see:

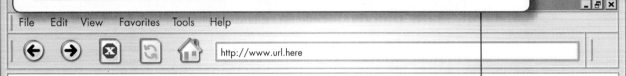

File   Edit   View   Favorites   Tools   Help

http://www.url.here

Birthday Traditions from Around the World

Discover how the tradition of birthdays started. Find out how people in other countries celebrate birthdays.

Birthday parties are always the highlight of a child's year, but did you ever wonder how the tradition of birthday parties started?

- How Birthday Parties Started
- **Birthdays in Different Countries**
- Tell Us About Your Family's Birthday Traditions
- See a Listing of Birthday Party Places
- Find a Birthday Present
- Find Out What Famous People Share Your Birth Date
- Children's Book and Video Store
- Birthday Related Products and Links
- Go to the Kids Parties Connection Home Page

You click on the link Birthdays in Different Countries. You can read about some of these traditions on the next page.

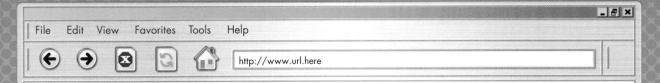

Birthdays in Different Countries

Canada—In some parts of Canada, birthday children get their noses greased for good luck. Greased noses make children too slippery for bad luck to catch them.

China—People are invited to lunch. Noodles are served to wish the birthday child a long life.

Cuba—The parties are similar to those in the United States. Food, decorations, gifts, piñatas, cake, candles, the "Happy Birthday" song, and games are included.

India—At school, the birthday child wears special clothing and passes out chocolates to the entire class.

Vietnam—Everyone's birthday is celebrated on New Year's Day, called Tet. The Vietnamese do not celebrate the exact day they were born. A baby turns one on Tet no matter when he or she was born that year.

Reading Across Texts
Compare the birthday celebration in *A Birthday Basket for Tía* to the ones listed above. Which is most like Tía's celebration? Which are most different?

Writing Across Texts Make a chart to show your comparisons.

Writing and Conventions

Writing Realistic Fiction

Prompt *A Birthday Basket for Tía* tells about a person finding the perfect present for a favorite aunt. Think about family celebrations. Now write a story about a character who is planning a family celebration.

Writing Trait

Words in **sentences** should be in an order that makes sense.

Student Model

Family Reunion

My family is planning a reunion for Sunday, June 29. We will meet in Kent, Ohio.

I will meet cousins I have never met before! We will play softball, volleyball, and soccer. Then we will have a picnic dinner.

I am excited that I get to help plan the family reunion!

The words in the sentences are in order.

Writer uses a comma between a city and state.

Realistic fiction has parts that can really happen.

LC1.2 Recognize and use the correct word order in written sentences. LC1.4 Use commas in the greeting and closure of a letter and with dates and items in a series.

Grammar Using Commas

Commas are used in addresses: San Antonio, TX 78250.

Commas are used in dates: May 2, 1939.

Commas are used to begin and end a letter.

Dear Cecilia,   Yours truly,

Commas are used to separate three or more things in a sentence: Walk, skip, or run.

Practice Look at the model. Write a quick note to your uncle telling him the date of the reunion. Begin and end the note properly. Use commas where they are needed.

Let's Talk About
Traditions

LS1.0 Students listen critically and respond appropriately to oral communication. They speak in a manner that guides the listener to understand important ideas by using proper phrasing, pitch, and modulation.

Build Vocabulary

Learn ◉ **Skill Suffixes** are word parts added to the ends of words to change their meanings. The meaning of a suffix can help you figure out what an unfamiliar word means. Two common suffixes are *-less* and *-able*.

> When the suffix *-less* is added to a word, it usually makes the word mean "without ____." For example, *cordless* means "without a cord."

> When the suffix *-able* (or *–ible*) is added to a word, it usually makes the word mean "able to ____." For instance *breakable* means "able to break."

Practice Read "Like a Cowboy" on page 413. Look for words that end in *-able, -less,* or other suffixes. Make a list of these words.

Words to Know	cowboy	cattle	campfire
	herd	trails	railroad
	galloped		

On Your Own Reread "Like a Cowboy." Write at least two sentences using words with suffixes. Then write three sentences using words from this week's Words to Know list.

R1.9 Know the meaning of simple prefixes and suffixes (e.g., *over-, un-, -ing, -ly*).
G3R1.7 Use a dictionary to learn the meaning and other features of unknown words.

LIKE A COWBOY

What was it like to be a cowboy long ago? To find out, some people stay on a ranch. They ride horses, and they chase and rope cattle, or cows. At night around a campfire, they tell stories and sing songs. They even take a herd of cattle on a cattle drive.

Long ago, cowboys took herds of cattle on cattle drives. They traveled on trails that ran from Texas to Kansas. From there, the railroad took the cattle to cities in the East. The trail was a thousand miles long. The cattle drive lasted for months.

The cattle drive at the ranch today lasts only a day or two. Still, the cattle drive gives people an idea of what it was like to be a cowboy. They can imagine how hard the fearless cowboys worked on the trail. They can imagine how happy the cowboys were as they galloped into a town after a long, uncomfortable cattle drive.

 Need a Review?
See *Words!*, p. W•6 for more information about suffixes.

 Ready to Try It?
Read *Cowboys* on pp. 416–437.

Build Comprehension

Learn  **⊙ Skill Cause and Effect**

- An *effect* is something that happens. A *cause* is why that thing happens.

- To understand causes and effects in your reading, ask yourself, "What happened?" and "Why did this happen?"

- Clue words such as *because, so*, and *since* can help you figure out what happened and why.

```
┌──────────┐        ┌──────────┐
│  What    │───────▶│  Why it  │
│ happened │        │ happened │
└──────────┘        └──────────┘
```

Practice   Read "The Stagecoach Driver" on page 415. Look for words that will help you see causes and effects.

On Your Own   **Write to Read** Reread "The Stagecoach Driver" and make a graphic organizer like the one above. Fill in your organizer to show what happened and why it happened. Then write a sentence of your own that tells a cause and effect.

COWBOYS

 Need a Review?
See *Picture It!* on p. PI•3 for more information about cause and effect.

 Ready to Try It?
As you read *Cowboys* on pp. 416–437, watch for clue words that will help you understand cause and effect relationships.

R2.4 Ask clarifying questions about essential textual elements of exposition (e.g., why, what if, how). **R2.6** Recognize cause-and-effect relationships in a text.

THE STAGECOACH DRIVER

Being a stagecoach driver was a hard job. A driver had to take care of a stagecoach full of people. A stagecoach would sometimes get stuck or tip over because it traveled on muddy trails and rocky roads. And sometimes stagecoaches were robbed.

Charley Parkhurst was a stagecoach driver. He was a small person with a patch over one eye. He did not talk much. Charley drove stagecoaches for 20 years. When he died, people found out that Charley was a woman!

Charlotte Parkhurst wanted to drive a stagecoach. But women were not allowed, so Charlotte changed her name to Charley. She put on men's clothes. For 20 years she acted like a man. No one knew her secret.

Skill Here is a clue word—*because*. It signals a cause and effect. It tells <u>why</u> stagecoaches sometimes got stuck or tipped over.

Skill Here is another clue word—*so*. Ask yourself, "Why did Charlotte change her name?"

Traditions

COWBOYS

by Lucille Recht Penner
illustrated by Ben Carter

Genre **Narrative nonfiction** gives information about the real world. Look for facts about cowboys.

What was it like to live as a cowboy?

If you were out west about a hundred years ago,
you might have heard a cowboy yelling—*ti yi yippy
yay!*—as he rode across the plains.

What was it like to be a cowboy way back then?
Cowboys lived on cattle ranches. A ranch had
a house for the rancher and his family, barns for
animals, and a bunkhouse where the cowboys slept.

The rancher owned thousands of cattle. They
wandered for miles looking for grass and water.

Twice a year, the cowboys drove all the cattle
together. This was called a roundup. The cowboys
counted the baby calves that had been born since
the last roundup. The biggest cattle were chosen to
sell at market.

A roundup was hard work. The cattle were wild and fast. They had long, sharp, dangerous horns. Cowboys called them Longhorns. If you made a Longhorn mad, it would charge at you. A cowboy didn't want to get close to an angry Longhorn.

So he made a loop in the end of his rope. Then he twirled it over his head and let it fly. When he caught the Longhorn, he could tell that it belonged to his ranch.

How could he tell? It was easy. Each rancher put a special mark called a brand on his cows. Baby calves didn't have brands, yet. They didn't need them. A baby calf always followed its mother.

Every ranch had its own name and its own brand. The Rocking Chair Ranch brand looked like a rocking chair. The Flying V Ranch brand looked like this: ᪣.

After the roundup was over, it was time to sell the Longhorns. That meant taking them to big market towns. Back then, there were no roads across the wide plains—only dusty trails that cattle had made with their hooves as they tramped along. Some trails were a thousand miles long! Since cattle could walk only fifteen miles a day, the long, hard trip often lasted months. It was called a trail drive. There was a lot to do to get ready.

At the beginning of a trail day, one cowboy rode out in front of the herd. "Come on, boys," he called

to the cattle. A few big Longhorns started after him. They bellowed and swung their heads from side to side. Other cattle followed, and soon they were all on their way.

Cattle didn't like so much walking. After a while, they wanted to turn around and go home. Cowboys rode up and down the sides of the herd to keep them in line. A few cowboys rode at the end of the herd to make sure no cattle were left behind.

It was hot on the trail. Cowboys wore hats
with wide brims to keep the sun out of their eyes.
When it rained, the brims made good umbrellas.
Around their necks, cowboys wore red bandannas.
When it got dusty, they pulled the bandannas
over their noses.

Leather leggings—called chaps—were tied over
their pants to keep out thorns and cactus spines.
High leather boots kept out dirt and pebbles.
Cowboy boots had handles called "mule ears."
The cowboy grabbed the mule ears to pull his
boots on.

What else did a cowboy need on his trail? A good horse. Cowboys spent the whole day on horseback. They rode little horses called cow ponies. A good cow pony was fearless. It could cross rough ground in the blackest night. It could swim a deep, wide river.

It could crash right through the bushes after a runaway cow. The cowboy had to hold on tight!

Every day the herd tramped the hot, dry plains. Two or three big steers were the leaders. They always walked in front. The cowboys got to know them well. They gave them pet names, like "Old Grumpy" and "Starface."

Cows could get in trouble. Sometimes one got stuck in the mud. The cowboy roped it and pulled it out. A cow might get hurt on the trail. A cowboy took care of that too.

At night the cowboys stopped to let the cattle eat, drink, and sleep. It was time for the cowboys to eat too. "Cookie" had a hot meal ready for them. That's what cowboys called the cook.

Cookie drove a special wagon called the chuckwagon. It had drawers for flour, salt, beans, and pots and pans. A water barrel was tied underneath.

Cookie gave every cowboy a big helping of biscuits, steak, gravy, and beans. He cooked the

same meal almost every night, but the cowboys didn't mind. It tasted good!

There were no tables or chairs, so the cowboys sat right on the ground. After dinner they played cards or read by the flickering light of the campfire. The nights were chilly and bright with stars.

But the cowboys didn't stay up late. They were
tired. At bedtime, they just pulled off their boots and
crawled into their bedrolls. A cowboy never wore
pajamas. What about a pillow? He used his saddle.

Trail drives were dangerous. Many things could
go wrong. The herd might stampede if there was
a loud noise—like a sudden crash of thunder.
A stampede was scary. Cattle ran wildly in all
directions, rolling their eyes and bellowing with fear.
The ground shook under them. The bravest cowboys
galloped to the front of the herd. They had to make

the leaders turn. They shouted at them and fired their six shooters in the air. They tried to make the cattle run in a circle until they calmed down.

Sometimes they'd run into rustlers. A rustler was a cow thief. Rustlers hid behind rocks and jumped out at the cattle to make them stampede. While the cowboys were trying to catch the terrified cattle and calm them down, the rustlers drove off as many as they could.

When the herd came to a big river, the cowboys in front galloped right into the water. The cattle plunged in after them. The cattle swam mostly under water. Sometimes the cowboys could see only the tips of their black noses and their long white horns.

Most cowboys didn't know how to swim. If a cowboy fell into the water, he grabbed the horse's tail and held on tight until they reached shore.

Trail drives often went through Indian Territory. The Indians charged ten cents a head to let the cattle cross their land. If the cowboys didn't pay, there might be a fight. But usually the money was handed over and the herd plodded on.

At last, the noisy, dusty cattle stamped into a market town. The cowboys drove them into pens near the railroad tracks. Then they got their pay. It was time for fun!

What do you think most cowboys wanted first? A bath! The barber had a big tub in the back of the shop. For a dollar, you could soak and soak. A boy kept throwing in pails of hot water. Ahh-h-h! Next it was time for a shave, a haircut, and some new clothes.

Tonight, the cowboys would sleep in real beds and eat dinner at a real table. They would sing, dance, and have fun with their friends.

But soon they would be heading back to Longhorn country. There would be many more hot days in the saddle. There would be many more cold nights under the stars.

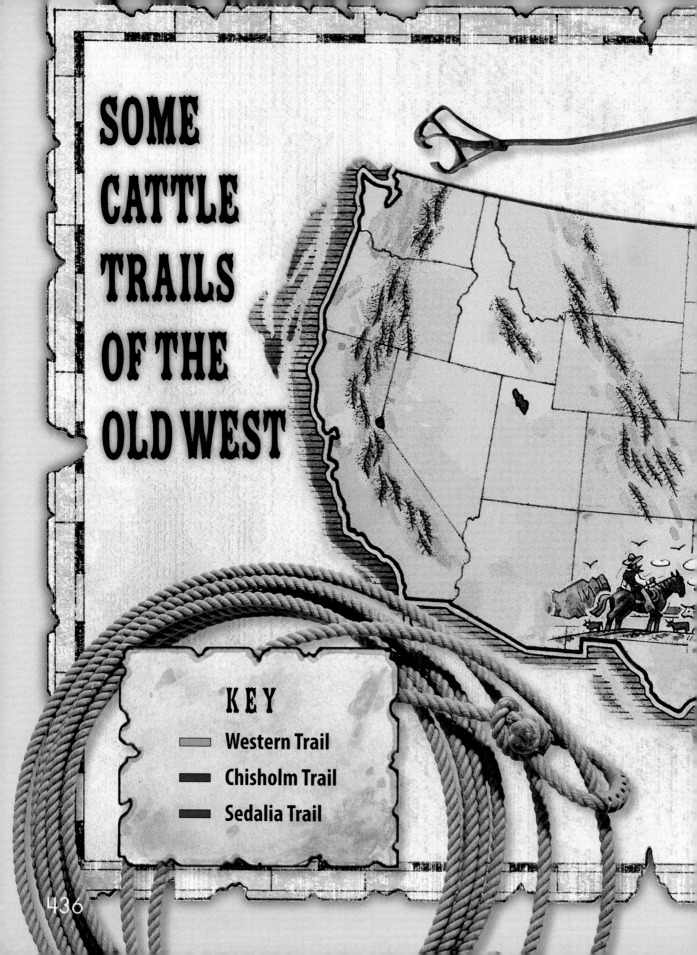

SOME CATTLE TRAILS OF THE OLD WEST

KEY

Western Trail

Chisholm Trail

Sedalia Trail

Nebraska
- Ogallala

Kansas
Ellsworth   Abilene

Dodge City

Missouri
- Sedalia

Arkansas

Oklahoma

Dallas

Texas

Louisiana

Houston

San Antonio

Brownsville

N
W · E
S

Think, Talk and Write

Talk About It Would you have liked a cowboy's job? What part would have been fun? What part might have made you pack up your gear and go away?

1. Use the pictures below to summarize what you learned. **Summarize**

2. What effect might a noisy thunderstorm have during a trail drive? Look back on pages 330 and 331 to help you answer. **Cause and Effect**

3. If you were to make a web to organize what you know about cowboys, what headings would you put in the main circle? in the smaller circles? **Graphic Organizers**

Look Back and Write Look back at the selection. What was it like to be a cowboy? Use details from the selection as you write your answer.

Summarize

R2.5 Restate facts and details in the text to clarify and organize ideas.
R2.6 Recognize cause-and-effect relationships in a text.

Meet the Author and the Illustrator

Lucille Recht Penner

Lucille Recht Penner often writes about life long ago. She likes to write about cowboys. People were adventurous and brave in the Old West. They were willing to do hard things even when they didn't know what would happen to them.

Ben Carter

Ben Carter has been an artist since he graduated from college. He is of Native American descent, and his books often draw upon his heritage.

Read other books written by Lucille Recht Penner or illustrated by Ben Carter.

X Marks the Spot!

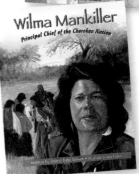

Wilma Mankiller: Principal Chief of the Cherokee Nation

Traditions

439

COWBOY GEAR

from *The Cowboy's Handbook*
★ by Tod Cody ★

A cowboy's clothes and equipment had to be hard-wearing. There was no room for luggage on the trail drive, and most cowboys wore the same thing for months. Mud-caked and smelly, these clothes were often burned at the end of the journey.

READY TO HIT THE TRAIL!

What to Wear When You're Riding the Range

HAT

You can use it to signal to other cowboys, beat trail dust off your clothes, and hold food for your horse. A true cowboy wears his hat when he's sleeping.

PANTS

Cowboys originally refused to wear jeans because they were worn by miners and farm laborers. Pants (trousers) made of thick woolen material are more comfortable to wear on horseback.

BOOTS

The pointed toes and high heels are designed for riding, not for walking. That's why cowboys in the movies walk the way they do!

BANDANNA

Soak it in water, roll it up into a wad, and place it under your hat to keep cool during a hot spell. You can also use it to filter muddy water and blindfold a "spooked" horse.

CHAPS

These thick leather leg-coverings will protect your legs from cow horns, rope burns, scrapes, and scratches. They also give a better grip to the saddle.

Reading Across Texts

What different information did each selection give about hats, bandannas, chaps, and boots?

Writing Across Texts

Write a paragraph explaining which piece of gear you think cowboys needed most.

Writing and Conventions

Writing Narrative Nonfiction

Prompt *Cowboys* describes a cowboy's job. Think about a job that you do at home or at school. Now write about how you do that job.

Student Model

Writer focuses on one main idea.

Writer uses a comma to combine sentences.

Narrative nonfiction tells about something real.

Washing Dishes

One of my jobs at home is washing the dishes. I fill the sink with water, and then I add the dish soap. It is easier to do the dishes right after dinner. Sometimes I leave them until the morning. Then I have to scrub hard, but I always am careful not to break a glass.

W1.1 Group related ideas and maintain a consistent focus.
LC1.2 Recognize and use the correct word order in written sentences.

Grammar Commas in Compound Sentences

Two sentences with ideas that go together can be combined using a comma and a connecting word, such as **and** or **but.** The combined sentence is called a **compound sentence.**

> A cow pony crossed rough ground.
> It swam deep rivers.

> A cow pony crossed rough ground,
> **and** it swam deep rivers.

Practice Look at the model. Write one of the compound sentences. Then write the sentence as two sentences without the comma and connecting word.

Let's Talk About
Traditions

LS1.0 Students listen critically and respond appropriately to oral communication. They speak in a manner that guides the listener to understand important ideas by using proper phrasing, pitch, and modulation.

Traditions

Build Vocabulary

Learn ⊙ **Skill Compound Words** are long words made up of smaller words put together. If you know the meanings of the smaller words, try putting them together to find the meaning of the compound word. For example, a *raincoat* is a coat we wear in the rain.

Practice Read "A Wedding Story" on page 447. Watch for this week's Words to Know. Which ones are compound words? Think about the meanings of the two smaller words in each compound. Then put the two meanings together. Does this help you understand the meaning of the compound word?

Words to Know	bridesmaids	midway	guest
	peers	insist	officially

On Your Own Reread "A Wedding Story." Make a list of all the compound words you find. Then write some sentences of your own using the compound words from your list.

R1.8 Use knowledge of individual words in unknown compound words to predict their meaning.

A Wedding Story

My Aunt Caroline is getting married. I am the flower girl. My job is to walk behind the bridesmaids and drop flower petals from a basket.

It is just like a fairy-tale wedding, except for one part. Midway through, a late guest comes in. When he opens the door, it is so loud everyone turns to look. But the wedding continues.

Now all the guests are going to a hotel ballroom for a big party. The bride and groom will ride in a long, black car. As Aunt Caroline gets in, I help make sure her dress is not caught in the door.

I go to wait in my mom's car. Then Uncle Adam peers. "You should be riding with us!" he says.

"Are you sure?" my mom asks.

"I insist," says Uncle Adam. He lifts me up and twirls me around. "Only the best for my new niece!"

I am glad Uncle Adam is officially part of our family.

 Need a Review?
See *Words!*, p. W•9 for more information about compound words.

 Ready to Try It?
Read *Uncle Peter's Amazing Chinese Wedding* on pp. 450–465.

Traditions

Build Comprehension

Learn ⊙ **Skill Draw Conclusions**

- When you read, you can draw conclusions, or figure out more about the characters and what happens in the story.

- Use what you have read and what you know about real life to ask or answer questions.

- Find words in the text to support your ideas.

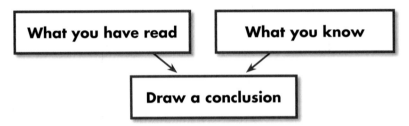

What you have read	What you know

Draw a conclusion

Practice Read "A New Baby" on page 449. Ask yourself questions to help you figure out more about the characters and what happens in the story.

On Your Own **Write to Read** Reread "A New Baby" and fill in a graphic organizer. Use information from the story and your own knowledge to draw conclusions. Then write a paragraph explaining what led to your conclusions.

UNCLE PETER'S AMAZING CHINESE WEDDING

❚❚ Need a Review?
See *Picture It!* on p. PI•7 for more information about drawing conclusions.

▷ Ready to Try It?
As you read about Uncle Peter's wedding on pp. 450–465, use what you know about feelings to help you draw conclusions.

R2.5 Restate facts and details in the text to clarify and organize ideas.
G3R2.2 Ask questions and support answers by connecting prior knowledge to literal information found in text.

A New Baby

Before Ben's sister was born, Ben was the baby of the family. He liked it that way. Mom took him to the library. Dad read him bedtime stories. Brother Chris played robots with him.

Now everyone is busy with the new baby. No one has time for robots or stories or trips to the park. Alone in his room, Ben wonders why everyone thinks baby Lily is so great. All she does is sleep and cry.

Chris comes in. "What's wrong, buddy?" he asks. Ben just shrugs.

"It's a little crazy here," Chris says. "But soon it will calm down. When you were a baby, I asked if we could give you back to the hospital."

"Really?" Ben asks.

"Yep. But Mom and Dad showed me how to hold you," Chris continues. "I told stories and sang you songs. I was first to make you laugh."

Ben starts to feel better. "Thanks, Chris. You're a good big brother."

Skill How is Ben feeling about the changes in his family? Use what you've read so far and what you know about real life to draw a conclusion.

Skill Can you draw a conclusion here? Ask yourself what happens to make Ben feel a little better.

UNCLE PETER'S AMAZING CHINESE WEDDING

古
囍
古

Written by Lenore Look
Illustrated by Yumi Heo

What is most amazing
about Uncle Peter's wedding?

This is Uncle Peter, my father's baby brother,
the coolest dude, a girl's best buddy.
Today he's getting married.

Everyone is happy happy. Everyone but me. This is
Saturday, and Uncle Peter should be with me, getting
dirty at the playground. I'm his special girl. *Just me.*
I am the jelly on his toast, and the leaves in his tea.
Now I am an umbrella turned inside out. I squeeze
back my tears.

It's the lucky hour for Uncle Peter to pick up his bride. If this were a hundred years ago, she would ride in a special chair carried by his friends. Two hundred years ago, he would carry her on his back. But today he is using his car.

"You can't see her yet," orders Cousin Mei-Ming, blocking Stella's door when we get there. "Pay up."

Now the groom must bargain for the bride, to show how much he'll give for her love. Until . . .

. . .here comes the bride! Amazing Stella, hair like unwoven silk, eyes like two black pearls, is dressed from head to toe in red red red to bring good luck. Dragons and phoenixes chase one another across her long, tall dress.

When Uncle Peter sees her, his face lights up like the aurora borealis and he reaches for her hand. I quickly grab the other one and pull.

"Let's go," I say.

Someone pushes me here and shoves me there, until we wind up inside Stella's house, and right in place for family pictures.

There is nowhere else to stand except around Stella. She is the sun, and we are the rest of the universe.

The camera follows Stella's every move. She twinkles and shines. I feel like cosmic dust.

The camera's flash explodes, and when I blink a lost tear slides down my cheek.

It rains birdseed and kisses when Stella and her bridesmaids, all the cousins, Uncle Peter, and I get back to his house.

"How about shooting a few hoops?" I shout to him, but he only laughs and winks at me. Why does he think I'm joking?

Inside, the bride and groom light incense and bow to the faded photographs of Ancient-Grandpa and Ancient-Grandma. They bow to the other grown-ups, then to each other.

457

It's time for the tea ceremony where the family officially welcomes the bride. Stella will serve tea, showing she is no longer a guest but a member of the family.

Suddenly I have an idea. I sneak into the kitchen where the hot Chrysanthemum Special is waiting in Grandma's fancy pot….

When Stella pours everyone asks, "What's this?" and peers into their tiny cups. It looks like water. It smells like water. It is water!

"Where's the *cha*?" Father wants to know and he hurries into the kitchen.

Mother looks straight at me. "Where's the tea?" she asks.

In a quiet room I tell my mother all my sadness.
Like water without tea leaves, it pours into her lap.
She tells me she will be sad, too, the day I leave her.
But, she says, she will also be happy, knowing I am
happy. Then gently, she kisses my head.

"I will never leave," I insist.

Hungbau, red packets of lucky money, pass into Stella's and Peter's hands as they share the freshly made tea. My aunties drape Stella with buttery gold jewelry to wish her health and happiness. Father, who is funny all the time, awards Stella with a shiny medal, for "Uncommon courage and bravery."

After the last drop of tea, Oldest Uncle writes Peter's Chinese name on a red cloth; then he writes Stella's. He gives them advice in Chinese, which sounds like a long, boring speech until midway through the speech Oldest Aunt clears her throat and gives him a little poke. The happy couple exchange rings. And then—yuck—they kiss. Everyone claps and smiles.

Stella changes into her dress for the banquet.
If this were a hundred years ago, she would change
into a hundred different dresses to show off her
family's wealth; if this were two hundred years ago,
she would have to change so many times that she
wouldn't be able to eat.

While Grandpa is saying that Stella's a feast for the eyes, I feast on vegetables, duck, and my favorite—long-life noodles, too slippery for chopsticks, but perfect to slurp from the edge of my plate. My favorite is the wedding soup, a sweet broth of red beans and pearl tapioca.

There are speeches to the bride and groom— Stella, award-winning science teacher, expert car mechanic, loving daughter, and Peter, the luckiest man in town.

Then Stella changes into her dancing dress. Everyone shimmies to a band called GingaDragonByte– even LoBaak, my great-grandmother, who can still get down at 103!

Before I get to dance with Uncle Peter, it's time to go. The good-bye line moves too slow for baby Henry, who's tired and cranky, but too fast for me.

Suddenly, "Come with me," someone says in my ear. It's Aunt Stella. "I nearly forgot the most important thing…," she says, pulling me outside.

Stella hands me a big box. "You are my first and only niece," she says. "I want you to do this." She dashes back to the line, but not before blowing me a kiss and saying, "I hope you know I love you."

I open the box a tiny bit. A butterfly flutters out, and then another. I open it all the way, and soon the air is filled with a thousand butterflies! The sight is so beautiful I can't even breathe.

Everyone has come to join me now. They gasp and clap and I take a deep bow, and finally everything feels like it should—like a wonderful dream.

"Great job, my awesome, special girl," I hear Uncle Peter say, and he scoops me into his arms.

Aunt Stella hugs us both. "Thank you for sharing your amazing uncle," she whispers just to me. Her good-bye dress looks like summer and she smells like trees and cartwheels.

"Welcome to the family," I whisper, and hug her back before they get in their car and drive away.

Think, Talk and Write

Talk About It Uncle Peter is very important to his niece. Tell about someone who is very important to you.

1. Use the pictures below to help you retell the story. **Retell**

2. Think about the things the girl does to try to get Uncle Peter's attention. What conclusions can you draw about how she feels about Uncle Peter's wedding? **Draw Conclusions**

3. What did you already know about weddings that helped you understand the story? **Prior Knowledge**

TEST PRACTICE ★ **Look Back and Write** Look back at the story. How did the girl's feelings about the wedding change? What are two things that made her feel better? Use details from the selection in your answer.

Retell

 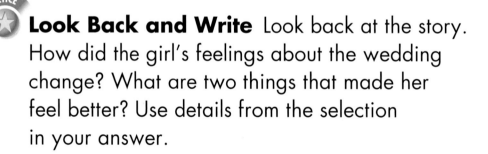 

LS1.7 Recount experiences in a logical sequence.
LS1.8 Retell stories, including characters, setting, and plot.

Meet the Author and the Illustrator

Lenore Look

Lenore Look is an award-winning author of children's books. She lives in New Jersey with her husband and children.

Yumi Heo

Yumi Heo was born and grew up in Korea, but came to the United States in 1989. Her illustrations have won awards. Ms. Heo lives near New York City with her husband and children.

Read more books by Lenore Look and Yumi Heo.

Love as Strong as Ginger

love as strong as ginger

lenore look ✷ stephen t. johnson

Henry's First Moon Birthday

Home Sweet Home

by Almira Astudillo Gilles

Long ago, there were no freeways or telephones, shopping malls or video games. Long ago, Native Americans were the only people in California.

Native Americans made many different kinds of homes, using materials that were easy to find. In the north, there were forests and plenty of wood for houses. The Miwok, a group that lived in Central California, had houses shaped like cones. Other houses, like those of the Chumash people of the

Chumash hut

south, were round. To build these round houses, poles made from branches were poked in the ground in a circle. These poles were bent at the top, and smaller branches were put around them. On the outside, pieces of bushes were added. A hole in the top let air inside. When it rained, the hole was covered with animal skin.

Inside a Native American house, you might see grass mats on the floor. You might see money made of sea snail shells. You might find moccasins and clothes of animal skins. You might find a bow and arrow for hunting. For children, there might be dolls or spinning tops made of acorns. Families lived together in one village.

moccasins

Grandparents, cousins, aunts, and uncles all lived nearby. Villages could be small, with just a few families, or large, with many families. Each village had a chief who could be a man or woman.

Many Native Americans in California used acorns for food. Some groups, like the Wiyot, lived far from the oak forests. They moved their homes into the forest when it was harvest time. Men shook the oak trees to make acorns fall. Women and children picked them up.

acorns

The most important thing about a Native American home was the family inside it. Just like today, a home was a place to rest and spend time together. These houses were one big room. Families played games. Elders told stories. Adults talked about important events in the village.

Native American men sometimes built a sweathouse. The sweathouse was a place men went to heal and to pray. Inside the sweathouse there was a fire pit with stones. With the fire burning, it became very hot inside. When the men became too sweaty, they ran outside and jumped into a cool creek.

A sweathouse is made this way:

Step 1. Make a frame out of long pieces of wood.

Step 2. Put branches across the frame.

Step 3. Put thick shrubs on top of the branches.

Step 4. Cover the roof with soil. The roof should be no more than five inches thick.

sweathouse

Reading Across Texts

Both "Home Sweet Home" and *Uncle Peter's Amazing Chinese Wedding* tell about families and cultural traditions. Find some words or sentences in each selection that show how the older members of a family help pass down traditions.

Writing Across Texts Write a brief paragraph that explains the role of elders in keeping traditions alive.

Writing and Conventions

Writing Realistic Fiction

Prompt In *Uncle Peter's Amazing Chinese Wedding*, a young girl feels neglected when her favorite uncle gets married. Think about other big changes that happen in families. Now write a realistic story about a family member experiencing a big change.

Writing Trait

Organize your writing with a beginning, middle, and end.

Student Model

The first sentence of a paragraph is indented.

Realistic fiction has parts that can be real.

The story is organized with a beginning, a middle, and an end.

When Grandma Came to Stay

When Kenny's grandma came to live with his family, everything changed. Kenny had to share his room with his baby sister. He had to be quiet in the afternoon because Grandma napped.

But soon Grandma started telling stories about when she was Kenny's age. Kenny realized she was just like him.

W1.1 Group related ideas and maintain a consistent focus. **W2.1** Write brief narratives based on their experiences: a. Move through a logical sequence of events. b. Describe the setting, characters, objects, and events in detail.

Grammar The Paragraph

A **paragraph** is a group of sentences about the same idea. The sentences are in an order that makes sense. One sentence gives the main idea. The other sentences give details about the main idea. The first sentence of a paragraph is indented.

Practice Copy the model. Circle the sentence that gives the main idea. Underline the sentences that give details.

Glossary

Aa

adventure (ad VEN cher) An **adventure** is an exciting or unusual thing to do: Riding a raft down the river was a great **adventure**. *NOUN*

afternoon (af ter NOON) The **afternoon** is the part of the day between morning and evening: On Saturday we played all **afternoon**. *NOUN*

angry (ANG gree) If you are **angry**, you feel upset or mad: Dad was **angry** when he saw the broken car window. *ADJECTIVE*

annoy (uh NOI) To **annoy** is to bother or make someone feel upset or angry: Please do not **annoy** others by talking during the movie. *VERB*

aunt (ANT or AHNT) Your **aunt** is your father's sister, your mother's sister, or your uncle's wife. *NOUN*

Bb

bank[1] (BANGK) A **bank** is a place where people keep their money: My brother has a **bank** for nickels and pennies. *NOUN*

bank[2] (BANGK) The **bank** of a river or lake is the ground beside it: He sat on the river **bank**. *NOUN*

bases (BAY sez)

1. A **base** is the bottom of something: The metal **bases** of the floor lamps might scratch the floor. *NOUN*

2. A **base** is also an object in some games: After hitting a home run, the player ran the **bases**. *NOUN*

basket (BASS kit)

1. A **basket** is something to carry or store things in: **Baskets** are made of straw, plastic, or other materials. *NOUN*

2. In basketball a **basket** is used as a goal: The **basket** is made of a metal ring with a net hanging from it. *NOUN*

basket

birthday (BERTH day) A **birthday** is the day that a person was born or something was started: Our country's **birthday** is July 4th. *NOUN*

blame (BLAYM) To **blame** is to hold someone responsible for something bad or wrong. *VERB*

blankets (BLANG kits) **Blankets** are soft, warm coverings for beds: We bought new **blankets** for our beds. *NOUN*

block (BLOK)

1. A **block** is a thick piece of wood or plastic: My little brother held one green **block** and two blue ones. *NOUN*

2. If you **block** something, you fill it so that nothing can pass by: I saw a large truck **block** traffic. *VERB*

3. A **block** is also an area of a city that has a street on each side: I walked down the **block** to my friend's house. *NOUN*

branches (BRANCH ez)

1. **Branches** are the part of the tree that grow out from the trunk: Swings hung from the trees' **branches**. *NOUN*

2. **Branches** are small parts of something: The **branches** of the river had calm water. *NOUN*

building

bridesmaids (BRIDEZ maydz) **Bridesmaids** are girls or women who help a bride on her wedding day. *NOUN*

building (BIL ding) A **building** is something that has been built: A **building** has walls and a roof. Schools, houses, and barns are **buildings**. *NOUN*

bumpy (BUHM pee) If something is **bumpy**, it is rough or has a lot of bumps: This sidewalk is too **bumpy** to skate on. *ADJECTIVE*

burning (BERN ing) **Burning** means to be on fire: The campers enjoyed watching the **burning** logs. *ADJECTIVE*

Cc

campfire (KAMP fyr) A **campfire** is an outdoor fire used for cooking or staying warm. *NOUN*

cattle (KAT uhl) **Cattle** are animals raised for their meat, milk, or skins: Cows and bulls are **cattle**. *NOUN PLURAL*

chased (CHAYST) When you **chase** someone or something, you run after it: The children **chased** the ball down the hill. *VERB*

cheers (CHEERZ) When you **cheer**, you call out or yell loudly to show you like something: She **cheers** for her team. *VERB*

chewing

chewing (CHOO ing) When you **chew** something, you crush it with your teeth: He was **chewing** the nuts. *VERB*

chuckle (CHUK uhl) When you **chuckle**, you laugh softly: She will **chuckle** when she sees her gift. _VERB_

climbed (KLYMD) When you **climb**, you go up something, usually by using your hands and feet: The children **climbed** into the bus. _VERB_

clubhouse (KLUB HOWSS) A **clubhouse** is a building used by a group of people joined together for some special reason. _NOUN_

clung (KLUNG)

1. If you **clung**, you held tightly to someone or something: He **clung** to his father's hand. _VERB_

2. **Clung** means to have stuck to something: The vine **clung** to the wall. _VERB_

collects (kuh LEKTS) If you **collect** things, you bring them together or gather them together: The student **collects** the crayons. _VERB_

complain (kuhm PLAYN) To **complain** is to say that you are unhappy about something: Some people **complain** about the weather. _VERB_

cowboy (KOW boi) A **cowboy** is a person who works on a cattle ranch: **Cowboys** also take part in rodeos. _NOUN_

cowboy

Dd

dripping (DRIP ing) When something **drips**, it falls in drops: The rain was **dripping** on the roof. *VERB*

Ee

exploring (ek SPLOR ing) When you are **exploring**, you are traveling to discover new areas: Astronauts are **exploring** outer space. *VERB*

Ff

fair¹ (FAIR) If you are **fair**, you go by the rules. People who are **fair** treat everyone the same: Try to be **fair** in everything you do. *ADJECTIVE*

fair² (FAIR) A **fair** is an outdoor show of farm animals and other things: We enjoyed ourselves at the county **fair**. *NOUN*

fair

favorite (FAY vuhr it)
1. Your **favorite** thing is the one you like better than all the others: What is your **favorite** color? *ADJECTIVE*

2. A **favorite** is a person or thing that you like very much: Pizza is a **favorite** with me. *NOUN*

field (FEELD) A **field** is a piece of land used for a special purpose: The football **field** needs to be mowed. *NOUN*

fingers (FING gerz) Your **fingers** are the five end parts of your hand. *NOUN*

fingers

flag

flag (FLAG) A **flag** is a piece of colored cloth with stars or other symbols on it: Every country and state has its own **flag**. *NOUN*

freedom (FREE duhm) **Freedom** is not being under someone else's control or rule. *NOUN*

fruit (FROOT) **Fruit** is the part of a tree, bush, or vine that has seeds in it and is good to eat: Apples, oranges, and strawberries are **fruit**. *NOUN*

fruit

Gg

galloped (GAL uhpt) To **gallop** is to run very fast: The horse **galloped** down the road. *VERB*

giant (JY uhnt)
1. In stories, a **giant** is a person who is very large. *NOUN*
2. If something is **giant**, it is much bigger than usual: We made a **giant** sandwich for lunch. *ADJECTIVE*

giant

grabbed (GRABD) When you **grab** something, you take it suddenly: The dog **grabbed** the bone. *VERB*

grains (GRAYNZ) **Grains** are tiny pieces or particles: There are millions of **grains** of sand on the beach. *NOUN*

greatest (GRAYT est) If something is the **greatest**, it is the best and most important: He thought it was the **greatest** book he had ever read. *ADJECTIVE*

Glossary

guest (GEST) A **guest** is someone who is invited to visit or attend an event: Each **guest** at my party wore a funny hat. *NOUN*

Hh

harvest (HAR vist)
1. A **harvest** is the ripe crops that are picked after the growing season is over: The corn **harvest** was poor after the hot, dry summer. *NOUN*
2. When you **harvest**, you gather in the crops and store them: We **harvest** the apples in late fall. *VERB*

herd (HERD) A **herd** is a group of the same kind of animals: We saw a **herd** of cows when we drove through the country. *NOUN*

herd

Ii

ideas (eye DEE uhz) **Ideas** are thoughts or plans: The class had different **ideas** on how to spend the money. *NOUN*

important (im PORT uhnt) Something that is **important** has a lot of meaning or worth: Learning to read is **important**. *ADJECTIVE*

insist (in SIST) If you **insist** on something, you state it firmly or demand it: I **insist** that you go first. *VERB*

Jj

jagged (JAG id) Something that is **jagged** is uneven and pointy or sharp: The glass broke into **jagged** pieces. *ADJECTIVE*

Mm

masks (MASKS) **Masks** are coverings that hide or protect your face: The firefighters wear **masks** to help them breathe. *NOUN*

midway (MID WAY) **Midway** means in the middle or half of the way: I met my friends **midway** between my house and school. *ADVERB*

mumbles (MUHM buhls) Someone who **mumbles** speaks too quietly to be heard clearly: When John **mumbles,** I can't understand what he is saying. *VERB*

Nn

nicknames (NIK naymz) **Nicknames** are names used instead of real names: Ed is a **nickname** for Edward. *NOUN*

Oo

officially (uh FISH uh lee) If something is done **officially,** it is done with approval from someone in charge: School was **officially** closed for the holidays. *ADVERB*

Pp

particles (PAR tuh kuhls) **Particles** are very tiny pieces: The table had **particles** of dust on top. *NOUN*

peers (PEERZ) To **peer** means to look carefully at something that is hard to see: The cat **peers** at the tiny ant crawling up the wall. *VERB*

picnic (PIK nik) A **picnic** is a party with a meal outdoors: Our class had a **picnic** at the park. *NOUN*

plate (PLAYT)

1. A **plate** is a dish that is almost flat and is usually round: We eat food from **plates**. NOUN

2. A **plate** is a hard rubber slab that a baseball player stands beside to hit the ball. NOUN

P.M. (PEE EM) These letters stand for *post meridiem,* which means "after midday." **P.M.** refers to the time between noon and 11:59 at night.

practice (PRAK tiss) A **practice** is a training session: Coach says that to play the game, you must go to **practice**. NOUN

present

present[1] (PREZ uhnt) Another word for **present** is *here.* If you are **present**, you are not absent: Every member of the class is **present** today. ADJECTIVE

present[2] (PREZ uhnt) A **present** is a gift. A **present** is something that someone gives you or that you give someone: His uncle sent him a birthday **present**. NOUN

pressing (PRESS ing)

1. **Pressing** is pushing something in a steady way: The child is **pressing** the elevator button. VERB

2. When you **press** clothes, you make them smooth with a hot iron: Dad was **pressing** my shirt to get out the wrinkles. VERB

pretended (pri TEND ed) To **pretend** is to make believe that something is real when it is not: We **pretended** that we were camping. VERB

Qq

quickly (KWIK lee) **Quickly** means in a short time: When I asked him a question, he answered **quickly**. *ADVERB*

quilt (KWILT) A **quilt** is a soft covering for a bed: A **quilt** is usually made from two pieces of cloth sewn together with soft material between them. *NOUN*

quilt

Rr

railroad (RAYL rohd) A **railroad** is a system of trains, tracks, stations, and other property run by a transportation company: The cattle pens were near the **railroad** tracks. *NOUN*

roar (ROR) A **roar** is a loud, deep sound: The **roar** of the lion frightened some people at the zoo. *NOUN*

root (ROOT) The **root** is the part of a plant that grows underground: A plant gets food and water through its **roots**. *NOUN*

Ss

sailed (SAYLD) When something **sails**, it travels on the water or through the air: The ball **sailed** out of the ballpark. *VERB*

seep (SEEP) To **seep** means to soak through or to pass through an opening very slowly in small amounts: Heavy rains caused water to **seep** into our basement. *VERB*

shrugs (SHRUHGZ) To **shrug** is to raise your shoulders briefly to show that you are not interested or do not know: Every time I ask my brother if he wants to play, he just **shrugs.** *VERB*

signature (SIG nuh chur) Your **signature** is the way you sign your name: Each student needed a parent's **signature** on the permission slip. *NOUN*

signmaker (SYN mayk er) A **signmaker** makes marks or words on a sign that give information or tell you what to do or not to do. *NOUN*

smooth (SMOOTH) When something is **smooth**, it has an even surface. Something that is **smooth** is not bumpy or rough: The road was very **smooth**. *ADJECTIVE*

soil

soil^1 (SOIL) **Soil** is the top layer of the earth. **Soil** is dirt: Our garden has such rich **soil** that almost anything will grow in it. *NOUN*

soil^2 (SOIL) If you **soil** something, you make it dirty: The dust will **soil** her white gloves. *VERB*

special (SPESH uhl)
1. If something is **special**, it is unusual or different in some way: Your birthday is a **special** day. *ADJECTIVE*
2. A **special** is a TV show produced for one showing: I saw a TV **special** on wolves. *NOUN*

stars (STARZ)

1. **Stars** are the very bright points of light that shine in the sky at night: On a clear night, the **stars** are very bright. *NOUN*

2. **Stars** are shapes that have five or six points: I drew **stars** on the paper. *NOUN*

station (STAY shuhn) A **station** is a building or place used for a special reason: The man went to the police **station**. *NOUN*

stripes (STRYPS) **Stripes** are long, narrow bands of color: Our flag has seven red **stripes** and six white **stripes**. *NOUN*

strong (STRAWNG) Something that is **strong** has power. A **strong** person can lift and carry things that are heavy. **Strong** means not weak: A **strong** wind blew down the tree. *ADJECTIVE*

stuffing (STUF ing) **Stuffing** is material used to fill or pack something: The **stuffing** is coming out of the pillow. *NOUN*

substances (SUHB stan sez) A **substance** is something that has weight and takes up space: Solids, liquids, and powders are examples of **substances.** *NOUN*

Tt

tears (TEERZ) **Tears** are drops of salty water that come from eyes: **Tears** fall when you cry. *NOUN*

texture (TEKS chur) **Texture** is the look and feel of something, especially its roughness or smoothness. *NOUN*

threw (THROO) When you **threw** something, you sent it through the air: She **threw** the ball back to him. *VERB*

threw

tightly (TYT lee) When something is tied **tightly**, it is firmly tied: The rope was tied **tightly** around the ladders on the truck. *ADVERB*

townspeople (TOWNZ pee puhl) **Townspeople** are the men, women, and children who live in a village or town: The **townspeople** enjoyed the fair. *NOUN*

trails (TRAYLZ) **Trails** are paths across fields or through the woods: Two **trails** led to the river. *NOUN*

treat (TREET) A **treat** is a gift of food, drink, a free ticket, or the like: She gave us **treats** on the last day of school. *NOUN*

trouble (TRUHB uhl)
1. **Trouble** is something that makes you upset, bothers you, or gives you pain: I had a lot of **trouble** working those math problems. *NOUN*

2. If you are in **trouble**, people are angry or upset with you: You will be in **trouble** if you knock that can of paint over. *NOUN*

truest (TROO ist) To be **true** is to be faithful and loyal: She is the **truest** friend I have. *ADJECTIVE*

486

trunks (TRUHNGKS) **Trunks** are large boxes for carrying clothes. *NOUN*

trunks

Uu

unpacked (uhn PAKT) To **unpack** is to take things out that were packed in a box, trunk, or other container: He **unpacked** his suitcase. *VERB*

Vv

vine (VYN) A **vine** is a plant that grows along the ground. Some **vines** climb up walls and fences: Pumpkins, melons, and grapes grow on **vines**. *NOUN*

Ww

wagged (WAGD) To **wag** is to move from side to side or up and down: The dog **wagged** her tail. *VERB*

wondered (WUHN derd) When you **wondered** about something, you wanted to know about it: He **wondered** what time it was. *VERB*

wrapped (RAPT) When you **wrap** something, you cover it up, usually with paper: We **wrapped** presents all morning. *VERB*

wrapped

Unit 4

The Quilt Story

English	Spanish
blankets	mantas
pretended	imaginó
quilt	edredón
stuffing	relleno
trunks	baúles
unpacked	desempacaron
wrapped	envolvió

Life Cycle of a Pumpkin

English	Spanish
bumpy	desiguales
fruit	fruta
harvest	cosecha
root	raíz
smooth	lisas
soil	tierra
vine	enredadera

Soil

English	Spanish
grains	granos
jagged	dentados
particles	*partículas
seep	se filtra
substances	*sustancias
texture	*textura

I Like Where I Am

English	Spanish
block	cuadra
chuckle	echan risitas
fair	justo
giant	enorme
strong	fuertes
tears	lágrimas
trouble	problemas

* English/Spanish Cognate: A **cognate** is a word that is similar in Spanish and has the same meaning in both languages.

Helen Keller and the Big Storm

English	Spanish
angry	enojada
branches	ramas
clung	se aferró
fingers	dedos
picnic	comida campestre
pressing	presionando
special	*especial

Unit 5

Fire Fighter!

English	Spanish
building	edificio
burning	ardiente
masks	máscaras
quickly	rápidamente
roar	rugido
station	*estación
tightly	firmemente

Carl the Complainer

English	Spanish
annoy	enojar
complain	quejarse
mumbles	dice entre dientes
P.M.	*P.M.
shrugs	se encoje de hombros
signature	firma

Bad Dog, Dodger!

English	Spanish
chased	persiguieron
chewing	mordiendo
dripping	goteando
grabbed	agarró
practice	entrenamiento
treat	galletas (de perro)
wagged	meneó

Horace and Morris but mostly Dolores

English	Spanish
adventure	*aventura
climbed	subieron
clubhouse	casa del club
exploring	*explorando
greatest	mejores
truest	más verdaderos
wondered	se preguntaba

The Signmaker's Assistant

English	Spanish
afternoon	tarde
blame	culpen
idea	*idea
important	*importante
signmaker	rotulista
townspeople	ciudadanos

Unit 6

Just Like Josh Gibson

English	Spanish
bases	*bases
cheers	gritos de entusiasmo
field	campo
plate	base
sailed	volaban
threw	tiró

Red, White, and Blue: The Story of the American Flag

English	Spanish
America	Estados Unidos
birthday	cumpleaños
flag	bandera
freedom	libertad
nicknames	apodos
stars	estrellas
stripes	franjas

A Birthday Basket for Tía

English	Spanish
aunt	tía
bank	alcancía
basket	cesta
collects	recoge
favorite	*favorito
present	regalo

Cowboys

English	Spanish
campfire	fuego (de campamento)
cattle	ganado
cowboy	vaquero
galloped	galoparon
herd	manada
railroad	ferrocarril
trails	sendas

Uncle Peter's Amazing Chinese Wedding

English	Spanish
bridesmaids	damas de honor
guest	invitada
insist	*insisto
midway	a la mitad
officially	*oficialmente
peers	mivra

Reading

1.0 Word Analysis, Fluency, and Systematic Vocabulary Development

Students understand the basic features of reading. They select letter patterns and know how to translate them into spoken language by using phonics, syllabication, and word parts. They apply this knowledge to achieve fluent oral and silent reading.

Decoding and Word Recognition

1.1 Recognize and use knowledge of spelling patterns (e.g., diphthongs, special vowel spellings) when reading.

1.2 Apply knowledge of basic syllabication rules when reading (e.g., vowel-consonant-vowel = *su/ per*; vowel-consonant/consonant-vowel = *sup/ per*).

1.3 Decode two-syllable nonsense words and regular multisyllable words.

1.4 Recognize common abbreviations (e.g., *Jan., Sun., Mr., St.*).

1.5 Identify and correctly use regular plurals (e.g., *-s, -es, -ies*) and irregular plurals (e.g., *fly/ flies, wife/ wives*).

1.6 Read aloud fluently and accurately and with appropriate intonation and expression.

Vocabulary and Concept Development

1.7 Understand and explain common antonyms and synonyms.

1.8 Use knowledge of individual words in unknown compound words to predict their meaning.

1.9 Know the meaning of simple prefixes and suffixes (e.g., *over-, un-, -ing, -ly*).

1.10 Identify simple multiple-meaning words.

2.0 Reading Comprehension

Students read and understand grade-level-appropriate material. They draw upon a variety of comprehension strategies as needed (e.g., generating and responding to essential questions, making predictions, comparing information from several sources). The selections in *Recommended Literature, Kindergarten Through Grade Twelve* illustrate the quality and complexity of the materials to be read by students. In addition to their regular school reading, by grade four, students read one-half million words annually, including a good representation of grade-level-appropriate narrative and expository text (e.g., classic and contemporary literature, magazines, newspapers, online information). In grade two, students continue to make progress toward this goal.

Structural Features of Informational Materials

2.1 Use titles, tables of contents, and chapter headings to locate information in expository text.

Comprehension and Analysis of Grade-Level-Appropriate Text

2.2 State the purpose in reading (i.e., tell what information is sought).

2.3 Use knowledge of the author's purpose(s) to comprehend informational text.

2.4 Ask clarifying questions about essential textual elements of exposition (e.g., *why, what if, how*).

2.5 Restate facts and details in the text to clarify and organize ideas.

2.6 Recognize cause-and-effect relationships in a text.

2.7 Interpret information from diagrams, charts, and graphs.

2.8 Follow two-step written instructions.

3.0. Literary Response and Analysis

Students read and respond to a wide variety of significant works of children's literature. They distinguish between the structural features of the text and the literary terms or elements (e.g., theme, plot, setting, characters). The selections in *Recommended Literature, Kindergarten Through Grade Twelve* illustrate the quality and complexity of the materials to be read by students.

Narrative Analysis of Grade-Level-Appropriate Text

3.1 Compare and contrast plots, settings, and characters presented by different authors.

3.2 Generate alternative endings to plots and identify the reason or reasons for, and the impact of, the alternatives.

3.3 Compare and contrast different versions of the same stories that reflect different cultures.

3.4 Identify the use of rhythm, rhyme, and alliteration in poetry.

Writing

1.0 Writing Strategies

Students write clear and coherent sentences and paragraphs that develop a central idea. Their writing shows they consider the audience and purpose. Students progress through the stages of the writing process (e.g., prewriting, drafting, revising, editing successive versions).

Organization and Focus

1.1 Group related ideas and maintain a consistent focus.

Penmanship

1.2 Create readable documents with legible handwriting.

Research

1.3 Understand the purposes of various reference materials (e.g., dictionary, thesaurus, atlas).

Evaluation and Revision

1.4 Revise original drafts to improve sequence and provide more descriptive detail.

2.0 Writing Applications (Genres and Their Characteristics)

Students write compositions that describe and explain familiar objects, events, and experiences. Student writing demonstrates a command of standard American English and the drafting, research, and organizational strategies outlined in Writing Standard 1.0.

Using the writing strategies of grade two outlined in Writing Standard 1.0, students:

2.1 Write brief narratives based on their experiences:

    a. Move through a logical sequence of events.

    b. Describe the setting, characters, objects, and events in detail.

2.2 Write a friendly letter complete with the date, salutation, body, closing, and signature.

Written and Oral English Language Conventions

The standards for written and oral English language conventions have been placed between those for writing and for listening and speaking because these conventions are essential to both sets of skills.

1.0 Written and Oral English Language Conventions

Students write and speak with a command of standard English conventions appropriate to this grade level.

Sentence Structure

1.1 Distinguish between complete and incomplete sentences.

1.2 Recognize and use the correct word order in written sentences.

Grammar

1.3 Identify and correctly use various parts of speech, including nouns and verbs, in writing and speaking.

Punctuation

1.4 Use commas in the greeting and closure of a letter and with dates and items in a series.

1.5 Use quotation marks correctly.

Capitalization

1.6 Capitalize all proper nouns, words at the beginning of sentences and greetings, months and days of the week, and titles and initials of people.

Spelling

1.7 Spell frequently used, irregular words correctly (e.g., *was, were, says, said, who, what, why*).

1.8 Spell basic short-vowel, long-vowel, *r*- controlled, and consonant-blend patterns correctly.

Listening and Speaking

1.0 Listening and Speaking Strategies

Students listen critically and respond appropriately to oral communication. They speak in a manner that guides the listener to understand important ideas by using proper phrasing, pitch, and modulation.

Comprehension

1.1 Determine the purpose or purposes of listening (e.g., to obtain information, to solve problems, for enjoyment).

1.2 Ask for clarification and explanation of stories and ideas.

1.3 Paraphrase information that has been shared orally by others.

1.4 Give and follow three- and four-step oral directions.

Organization and Delivery of Oral Communication

1.5 Organize presentations to maintain a clear focus.

1.6 Speak clearly and at an appropriate pace for the type of communication (e.g., informal discussion, report to class).

1.7 Recount experiences in a logical sequence.

1.8 Retell stories, including characters, setting, and plot.

1.9 Report on a topic with supportive facts and details.

2.0 Speaking Applications (Genres and Their Characteristics)

Students deliver brief recitations and oral presentations about familiar experiences or interests that are organized around a coherent thesis statement. Student speaking demonstrates a command of standard American English and the organizational and delivery strategies outlined in Listening and Speaking Standard 1.0.

Using the speaking strategies of grade two outlined in Listening and Speaking Standard 1.0, students:

2.1 Recount experiences or present stories:

    a. Move through a logical sequence of events.

    b. Describe story elements (e.g., characters, plot, setting).

2.2 Report on a topic with facts and details, drawing from several sources of information.

Acknowledgments

Text

Page 30: *The Quilt Story* by Tony Johnston and illustrated by Tomie dePaola. Text Copyright © Tony Johnston, 1985. Illustrations Copyright © Tomie de Paola, 1985. Published by arrangement with G.P. Putnam's Sons, a division of Penguin Young Readers Group, A member of Penguin Group (USA) Inc., 345 Hudson Street, New York, NY 10014. All rights reserved.

Page 62: From *The Life Cycle of a Pumpkin* by Ron Fridell and Patricia Walsh. Copyright © 2001 Harcourt Education, Ltd. Used by permission.

Page 78: "How Do Seeds Know Which Way Is Up?" from *Where Fish Go in Winter and Other Great Mysteries* by Amy Goldman Koss, copyright © 1987 by Amy Goldman Koss. Used by permission of Dial Books for Young Readers, A Division of Penguin Young Readers Group, A Member of Penguin Group (USA) Inc., 345 Hudson Street, New York, NY 10014. All rights reserved.

Page 88: From *Soil* by Sally Walker. Copyright © 2007 by Sally Walker. All rights reserved. No part of this book may be reproduced or transmitted in any form or by any means, electronic or mechanical, including photocopying, recording, or by any information storage or retrieval system, without permission in writing from the publisher. Reprinted by permission of Lerner Publishing Group, Inc.

Page 120: *I Like Where I Am* by Jessica Harper and illustrated by Brain Karas. Text Copyright © Jessica Harper 2004. Illustrations Copyright © Brain Karas, 2004. Published by arrangement with G.P. Putnam's Sons, a division of Penguin Young Readers Group, A member of Penguin Group (USA) Inc., 345 Hudson Street, New York, NY 10014. All rights reserved.

Page 150: Reprinted with the permission of Aladdin Paperbacks, an imprint of Simon & Schuster Children's Publishing Division from *Helen Keller and the Big Storm* by Patricia Lakin. Copyright © 2002 Patricia Lakin.

Page 166: Reprinted with the permission of Aladdin Paperbacks, an imprint of Simon & Schuster Children's Publishing Division from *Wind* by Marion Dane Bauer. Copyright © 2003 Marion Dane Bauer.

Page 180: *Fire Fighter!* by Angela Royston. Copyright © 1998 Dorling Kindersley Limited, London. Reprinted by permission.

Page 208: From *Carl the Complainer* by Michelle Knudsen. Text copyright © 2005 by Kane Press, Inc. Illustrations copyright © 2005 by Maryann Cocca-Leffler. All rights reserved. No part of this book may be reproduced or transmitted in any form or by any means, electronic or mechanical, including photocopying, recording, or by any information storage or retrieval system, without permission in writing from the publisher. This edition published by arrangement with Kane Press, Inc. New York, NY, represented by Lerner Publishing Group, Inc.

Page 228: "Hard to Please" from *Falling Up* by Shel Silverstein. Copyright © 1996 by Shel Silverstein. Used by permission of HarperCollins Publishers.

Page 228: "Sour Face Ann" from *A Light in the Attic* by Shel Silverstein. Copyright © 1981 by Evil Eye Music, Inc. Used by permission of HarperCollins Publishers.

Page 238: Reprinted with the permission of Margaret K. McElderry Books, an imprint of Simon & Schuster's Children's Publishing Division from *Bad Dog, Dodger!* by Barbara Abercrombie. Text copyright © 2002 Barbara Abercrombie.

Page 266: From *Horace and Morris But Mostly Dolores* by James Howe, illustrated by Amy Walrod. Text copyright © 1999 by James Howe, Illustrations copyright © 1999 by Amy Walrod. Reprinted with permission of Atheneum Books for Young Readers, an Imprint of Simon & Schuster Children's Publishing Division. All rights reserved.

Page 298: *The Signmaker's Assistant* by Tedd Arnold. Copyright © 1992 by Tedd Arnold. Published by arrangement with Dial Books for Young Readers, A Division of Penguin Young Readers Group, A Member of Penguin Group (USA) Inc., 345 Hudson Street, New York, NY 10014. All rights reserved.

Page 316: Action Without Borders Web site, www.idealist.org/kt/youthorgs.html. Reprinted by permission.

Page 330: From *Just Like Josh Gibson* by Angela Johnson, illustrated by Beth Peck. Text copyright © 2004 by Angela Johnson, Illustrations copyright © 2004 by Beth Peck. Reprinted with permission of Simon & Schuster Books For Young Readers, an Imprint of Simon & Schuster Children's Publishing Division. All rights reserved.

Page 358: *Red, White, And Blue* by John Herman, and illustrated by Robin Roraback. Text Copyright © John Herman, 1998. Illustrations Copyright © Robin Roraback, 1998. Published by arrangement with Grosset & Dunlap, a division of Penguin Young Readers Group, a member of Penguin Group (USA) Inc., 345 Hudson Street, New York, NY 10014. All rights reserved.

Page 388: From *A Birthday Basket for Tía* by Pat Mora, illustrated by Cecily Lang. Text copyright © 1992 by Pat Mora, Illustrations copyright © 1992 by Cecily Lang. Reprinted with permission of Simon & Schuster Books For Young Readers, an Imprint of Simon & Schuster Children's Publishing Division. All rights reserved.

Page 404: From www.kidparties.com/traditions.htm. Reprinted by permission.

Page 416: *Cowboys* by Lucille Recht Penner. Text Copyright © Lucille Recht Penner, 1996. Illustrations Copyright © Ben Carter, 1996. Published by arrangement with Grosset & Dunlap, a division of Penguin Young Readers Group, a member of Penguin Group (USA) Inc. All rights reserved.

Page 440: From *The Cowboy's Handbook* by Tod Cody, copyright © 1966 by Breslich & Foss. Used by permission of Cobblehill Books, an affiliate of Dutton Children's Books, A Division of Penguin Young Readers Group, A Member of Penguin Group (USA) Inc., 345 Hudson Street, New York, NY 10014. All rights reserved.

Page 450: From *Uncle Peter's Amazing Chinese Wedding* by Lenore Look, illustrated by Yumi Heo. Text copyright © 2005 by Lenore Look, Illustrations copyright © 2005 by Yumi Heo. Reprinted with permission of Atheneum Books for Young Readers, an Imprint of Simon & Schuster Children's Publishing Division. All rights reserved.

Illustrations

Cover: Scott Gustafson
Pl•1-Pl•13 Robert Neubecker
87 Adam Benton
88 Nancy Woodman
137, 196-199, 238-251, 345, 439 Laura Ovresat
150-162 Troy Howell
213 Maryann Cocca-Leffler
346-349 Clint Hansen
358-374 Shannon Stirnweiss
W•2-W•15 Alessia Girasole

Photographs

Every effort has been made to secure permission and provide appropriate credit for photographic material. The publisher deeply regrets any omission and pledges to correct errors called to its attention in subsequent editions.

Unless otherwise acknowledged, all photographs are the property of Pearson Education, Inc.

Photo locators denoted as follows: Top (T), Center (C), Bottom (B), Left (L), Right (R), Background (Bkgd)

16 ©Mark A. Schneider/Visuals Unlimited
22 (Bkgd) ©Douglas Peebles Photography/Alamy
23 (T) ©Tony Freeman/PhotoEdit, (CR) ©Michael Habicht/Animals Animals/Earth Scenes
24 (C) ©Walter Hodges/Corbis
25 (TR) ©PM Images/Getty Images, (C) ©Steven Georges/Press-Telegram/Corbis
26 ©Michael Boys/Corbis
29 ©JLP/Jose L. Pelaez/Corbis
48 (BR) Getty Images
49 (TR) ©Best Read Guide/Cape Cod Travel, (CR, BR) Getty Images
50 (TR, BR) ©Best Read Guide/Cape Cod Travel
51 ©Lee Snider/Corbis
52 ©Amy Dykens/Best Read Guide/Cape Cod Travel
53 ©Best Read Guide/Cape Cod Travel
56 ©Superstudio/Getty Images
57 (T) ©Macduff Everton/Corbis, (C) ©Helmut Meyer zur Capellen/zefa/Corbis, (BR) ©2005/Ben Klaffke
58 (BR) Getty Images
59 (TR) Getty Images
62 (TR) ©Royalty-Free/Corbis, (Bkgd) Getty Images
64 (TC) ©2005 Ben Klaffke, (CR) ©Royalty-Free/Corbis
65 (R) ©Dwight R. Kuhn, (L) Getty Images
66 (R, L) ©Dwight R. Kuhn
67 (T) ©Shmuel Thaler/Index Stock Imagery
68 (T) ©Steve Solum/Index Stock Imagery
69 (T) ©Dwight R. Kuhn
70 (T) ©2005/Ben Klaffke
71 (T) ©Reuters/Corbis, (CR) ©Dwight R. Kuhn
72 (T) ©Dwight R. Kuhn, (CR) Getty Images
73 (T) ©Barry Lewis/Corbis, (CR) ©Matthew Klein/Corbis
74 (TR) ©Royalty-Free/Corbis, (TL) ©Tony Freeman/PhotoEdit

75 ©Richard Hamilton Smith/Corbis
79 ©David Aubrey/Corbis
81 ©Royalty-Free/Corbis
82 ©Tom McHugh/Photo Researchers, Inc.
83 (TR) ©Robert J. Erwin/Photo Researchers, Inc., (C) ©Richard T. Nowitz/Corbis, (BR) ©Michael Boys/Corbis
85 ©Peter Dazeley/zefa/Corbis
88 (Inset, Bkgd) Getty Images
90 ©Image Source
91 (T) ©Michael Habicht/Animals Animals/Earth Scenes, (CR) ©Peter Gould/OSF/Animals Animals/Earth Scenes
92 (B) ©Marli Miller/Visuals Unlimited
93 (TR) ©Robert & Jean Pollock/Visuals Unlimited, (TL) ©Paul Springett/Alamy
94 (T) ©Douglas Peebles Photography/Alamy
95 (CR) ©Mark A. Schneider/Visuals Unlimited, (B) Harry Taylor/©DK Images
96 (T) ©Peter Arnold, Inc./Alamy Images, (CR) ©Dennis Kunkel/Phototake
97 (B) ©Jacana/Photo Researchers, Inc.
98 (Inset) ©Kenneth W. Fink/Photo Researchers, Inc., (B) ©Michael S. Yamashita/Corbis
99 ©Marli Miller/Visuals Unlimited
102 (T) ©Aldo Pavan/Grand Tour/Corbis
103 (T) ©age fotostock/SuperStock
105 ©Michael Boys/Corbis
108 (T) ©Corbis/Jupiter Images, (BR) ©Tom McHugh /Photo Researchers, Inc.
109 (T) ©David K. Werk/Alamy, (BR) ©Corbis/Jupiter Images
110 (T) ©W. Perry Conway/Corbis, (BR) ©Arthur Morris/Corbis
111 (C) ©Corbis/Jupiter Images
113 ©Michael Habicht/Animals Animals/Earth Scenes
114 ©Ashley Cooper/Corbis
115 (TR) Corbis, (C) ©Jupiter Images
116 (BR) Getty Images
117 (TR) Corbis
119 Jupiter Images
138 ©Craig Aurness/Corbis
144 Index Open
145 (T) ©Andrew Holbrooke/Corbis, (C) ©Jim Zuckerman/Corbis
146 Getty Images
147 (TR) ©Amit Gupta/Reuters/Corbis, (CR) Getty Images
149 ©DK Images
152 (TR) ©Royalty-Free/Corbis, (BL) Getty Images
153 (BR) ©Bettmann/Corbis
154 (TL) Getty Images, (CL) ©Bettmann/Corbis
155 (TR, T) Getty Images, (C) Bettman/Corbis
157 (B) ©Royalty-Free/Corbis
159 ©Macduff Everton/Corbis
163 (TC) ©Royalty-Free/Corbis, (R) Getty Images, (C) Corbis
164 (BR) ©Royalty-Free/Corbis
167 (CR) ©Geostock/Getty Images, (BL) ©Martin Barraud/Getty Images
168 (TR) Getty Images, (TL) ©Michael Melford/Getty Images, (TC) ©Guy Grenier/Masterfile Corporation, (CL) ©Alan R. Moller/Getty Images, (BR) ©Randy Faris/Corbis, (BL) ©Guy Motil/Corbis
169 (TR) ©Stan Osolinski/Getty Images, (CR) Getty Images, (CL) ©World Perspectives/Getty Images, (Bkgd) ©Stephen Frink/Getty Images
170 (TR) ©Bettmann/Corbis
174 ©Ariel Skelley/Corbis
175 (TR) ©David Young-Wolff/Alamy Images, (CL) Getty Images, (BR) ©Lynton Gardiner/©DK Images
177 ©Tim Ross/Index Stock Imagery
179 ©image100/Jupiter Images
180 (C) ©Tim Ross/Index Stock Imagery
182 (TL) ©Roberts Company, Inc., (TC) Lynton Gardiner/©DK Images, (BL) ©Royalty-Free/Corbis
183 (R) ©DK Images, (BC) Getty Images
184 (TR, BR) ©DK Images
185 (TR) Lynton Gardiner/©DK Images
186 (C) Lynton Gardiner/©DK Images
188 (C) ©James McLoughlin
189 (BR) ©Rubberball Productions/Getty Images, (BC) Corbis
190 (B) Getty Images
191 (C) Lynton Gardiner/©DK Images
192 (TL, BR, BL) Lynton Gardiner/©DK Images
193 (T) Getty Images
194 Getty Images
195 (C) ©Richard Leeney/©DK Images
196 (TC) ©Roberts Company, Inc., (Bkgd) ©Comstock Images/Getty Images
197 (BR) ©Royalty-Free/Corbis
200 ©Rubberball Productions/Getty Images
201 ©DK Images
202 (C) ©David Young-Wolff/Alamy Images, (BR) ©Clark Brennan/Alamy Images, (Bkgd) Getty Images
203 (C) ©Scott Stulberg/Corbis
204 ©Royalty-Free/Corbis
232 ©Bob Sacha/Corbis

233 (TR) Corbis, (C) ©Michael Keller/Corbis
235 Getty Images
237 Getty Images
255 (TR) ©Cydney Conger/Corbis, (BR) ©Tracy Morgan/©DK Images, (BL) ©Jim Craigmyle/Corbis
256 (T) ©Jim Craigmyle/Corbis, (BC) ©Burke/Triolo Productions/FoodPix/Jupiter Images
257 (T) ©Jim Craigmyle/Corbis, (B) ©Tracy Morgan/©DK Images
260 (C) ©Janet Jarman/Corbis, (B) ©David Young-Wolff/PhotoEdit
261 (T) ©Simon D. Warren/zefa/Corbis
263 (Bkgd) ©Micha Pawlitzki/zefa/Corbis
265 (T, CR) Treehouse at Nay Aug Park built by Forever Young Treehouses, Inc. Photo by Jason DeBiasi/Courtesy of The City of Scranton, PA
286 (C) ©Bob Thomas/Getty Images
287 (C) ©Lori Adamski Peek/Getty Images, (BR) ©Bob Gomel/Corbis
288 (TR) ©Tim Pannell/Corbis, (BR) ©Charles Gupton/Corbis
289 ©Lori Adamski Peek/Getty Images
292 (R) ©Jerzyworks/Masterfile Corporation, (L) ©Masterfile Royalty-Free
293 ©Radius Images/Jupiter Images
294 ©James Nazz/Corbis
297 ©ClassicStock/Alamy Images
316 ©Tom Stewart/Corbis
317 (TR) Getty Images, (CR) Jacob Taposchaner/Taxi/Getty Images
324 Warren Faidley/Weatherstock, (R) ©Richard Hutchings/Photo Researchers, Inc., (L) ©David Schmidt/Masterfile Corporation
325 (T) ©Stan Liu/Icon SMI/Corbis
326 ©SuperStock/Alamy Images
327 Corbis
347 Library of Congress
352 (C) ©Joe Giza/Reuters/Corbis, (BR) ©Blend Images/Jupiter Images
353 (C) ©Ali Kabas/Alamy Images
354 ©Jerry Tobias/Corbis
357 (BR) ©Jim Cummins/Corbis
362 (TR) ©Bettmann/Corbis, (CR) ©PoodlesRock/Corbis, (BL) Stock Montage Inc.
366 (T) Composite photograph of the almost 200-year-old Star Spangled Banner, the flag that inspired the national anthem. Smithsonian's National Museum of American History, ©2004
367 (CR) Getty Images, (C) Corbis
368 (T) The Granger Collection, NY
370 ©Bjorn G. Bolstad/Photo Researchers, Inc.
372 (BL) Corbis
375 Digital Vision
378 ©Terence Beddis/Getty Images
381 (BR) ©Bettmann/Corbis, (BL) Stock Montage Inc.
382 ©Jennie Woodcock/Reflections Photolibrary/Corbis
383 (T) ©Richard Levine/Alamy Images, (CL) ©David Taylor/Alamy Images
402 (B) ©Jules Frazier/Getty Images
404 ©JLP/Jose L. Pelaez/Corbis
406 Getty Images
410 (C) ©David Stoecklein/Corbis, (BR) ©Jim Cummins/Corbis
411 (T) ©David Stoecklein/Corbis, (C) Jupiter Images
412 (BR) ©Macduff Everton/Corbis
413 (TR) ©Jules Frazier/Getty Images
415 (CR) Corbis
416 (C) ©Guillaud Jean Michel/Sygma/Corbis
435 (C) Getty Images
436 (T) ©Jules Frazier/Getty Images, (BL) Getty Images
437 (TR) ©Jules Frazier/Getty Images
438 ©Jules Frazier/Getty Images
440 (TR) ©C Squared Studios/Getty Images, (T) Getty Images, (BR) Brand X Pictures
444 ©Marilyn Angel Wynn/Nativestock Pictures/Corbis
445 (T) ©Richard Levine/Alamy Images, (L) ©Tim Mantoani/Masterfile Corporation
446 Jupiter Images
447 Jupiter Images
449 ©Owen Franken/Corbis
469 (T) ©Marilyn Angel Wynn/Nativestock Pictures/Corbis, (BL) ©The Bridgeman Art Library/Getty Images
470 (TR) Getty Images
471 (C) Indian Sweat House, Mendocino County, CA by Carleton Watkins, 1861-1871, #H87.204/19/State Library of Victoria, Melbourne, Australia
475 (T) ©Thinkstock/Getty Images
476 (TL) ©Craig Aurness/Corbis, (BL) image100
478 (CL) ©Patrick Ward/Corbis, (BR) Getty Images
479 (TR) Getty Images, (CR) ©Brian Hagiwara/Getty Images
480 (C) Getty Images
482 Getty Images
483 Getty Images
484 David Aubrey/Corbis
487 (TR) Corbis, (BR) ©Jose Luis Pelaez, Inc./Corbis
488 (BR) Tony Freeman/PhotoEdit

WORDS!

A Vocabulary Handbook

Antonyms

Antonyms are words that have opposite meaning. *Messy* and *neat* are antonyms.

Synonyms

Synonyms are words that have the same meaning or similar meaning. *Happy* and *glad* are synonyms.

Happy

Glad

Knowing and using synonyms can help make your writing more interesting. Look in a thesaurus to find synonyms.

Base Words

A base word is a word that cannot be broken down into smaller words or word parts. *Appear* and *cloud* are base words.

Appear

Knowing the meaning of a base word can help you understand the meaning of longer words.

Cloud

Prefixes

A prefix is a word part that can be added to the beginning of a base word. In the word *disappear, dis-* is a prefix.

Appear

Disappear

Knowing the meaning of a prefix can help you figure out the meaning of the new word.

Common Prefixes and Their Meanings

un-	not
re-	again, back
in-	not
dis-	not, opposite of
pre-	before

Suffixes

A suffix is a word part added to the end of a base word. In the word *cloudless*, *-less* is a suffix.

Cloud

Cloudless

Common Suffixes and Their Meanings

-able	can be done
-ment	action or process
-less	without
-tion	act, process

Knowing how a suffix changes a word can help you figure out the meaning of the new word.

Context Clues

Read the words before and after a word that you don't know to help you make sense of it.

I saw a robin, a bluebird, a sapsucker, and a turkey while walking in the woods.

Word Families

Word families are related words that have the same base word. Bicycle, recycle, and cyclone belong to the same word family. They all have the base word *cycle*.

Bicycle

Cyclone

Recycle

If you know what the base word means, you may be able to figure out the meaning of words related to it.

Compound Words

Compound words are words made of two smaller words. *Goldfish* and *basketball* are compound words.

gold + fish = goldfish

Look for smaller words that you already know in unfamiliar words.

basket + ball = basketball

Multiple-Meaning Words

Multiple-meaning words are words that can have different meanings depending on how they are used.

Homographs

Homographs are words that are spelled the same. They have different meanings, and they may be pronounced the same way or differently.

Bow

Bow

Read the words before and after a homograph to discover its meaning and pronunciation. Check a dictionary to be sure.

Homonyms

Homonyms are words that are spelled the same. They have different meanings, and they are pronounced the same way.

Pen

Pen

You can figure out the meaning of a homonym by reading the words around it.

Homophones

Homophones are words that sound the same, but they are spelled differently and they have different meanings.

Night

Knight

Homophones might be confusing when you hear them being read aloud. Pay attention to the words before and after the homophone to find its meaning.

Understanding
Homographs, Homonyms, and Homophones

	Pronunciation	Spelling	Meaning
Homographs	may be the same or different	same	different
Homonyms	same	same	different
Homophones	same	different	different

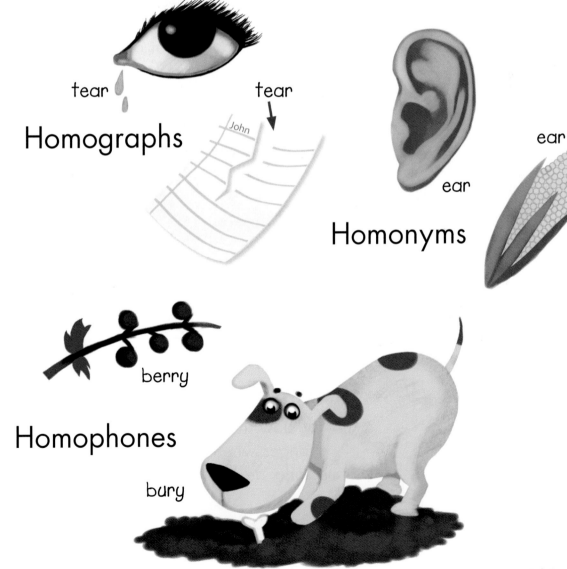

Homographs

tear

tear

John

Homonyms

ear

ear

Homophones

berry

bury

Dictionary

A dictionary is a book that explains the words of our language. The words in a dictionary are in alphabetical order.

continue: ❶ (kuhn TIN yoo)
❷ 1. If you continue doing something, you keep on going and do not stop: ❸ *These roads continue for miles.* ❹ [verb]
   2. To continue also means to go on with something after stopping for a while: *The teacher said that she would continue the story tomorrow.* [verb]
❺ -**continues, continued, continuing.**

❶ This part of the entry shows you how to pronounce the word.

❷ Here is the word's definition.

❸ The word is used in an example to help you understand its meaning.

❹ The dictionary entry tells you the word's part of speech. *Continue* is a verb.

❺ See how the word changes when it has a suffix added.

Thesaurus

A thesaurus is a book of synonyms. The words in a thesaurus are in alphabetical order.

sleep verb

be asleep, nap, doze, snooze, catch a few z's, take a siesta, catnap

Keep a thesaurus handy when you write. It can help you find just the right word.